ISLANDS TO THE WINDWARD

FIVE GEMS OF THE CARIBBEAN

Brian Dyde

CARIBBEAN

To my mother and father
Who have never visited any of these islands, but who made it
possible for me to appreciate them.

First published 1987

Published by *Macmillan Publishers Ltd*
London and Basingstoke
Associated companies and representatives in Accra,
Auckland, Delhi, Dublin, Gaborone, Hamburg, Harare,
Hong Kong, Kuala Lumpur, Lagos, Manzini, Melbourne,
Mexico City, Nairobi, New York, Singapore, Tokyo

ISBN 0–333–43936–8

Printed in Hong Kong

British Library Cataloguing in Publication Data
Dyde, Brian
  Islands to the windward: five gems of
  the Caribbean. — (Macmillan Caribbean
  guides)
  1. Leeward Islands (West Indies) —
  Description and travel — Guide-books
  I. Title
  917.297′04   F2006
ISBN 0-333-43936-8

Contents

Maps

Maps drawn by the author

Photographic acknowledgements

The author and publishers wish to acknowledge, with thanks, the following photographic sources:

Anne Bolt pp 5; 12 bottom; 25; 29 bottom; 42; 44; 62; 66; 68; 72; 78; 80; 82; Michael Bourne pp 3; 10; 15; 18; 41; 48 top and bottom; 52 bottom; Paddy Browne p 114; Brian Dyde pp 27; 61; 64; 65; 67; 83; 85; 95; 98; 107; 110; 112; G.W. Lennox pp 7; 20; 29 top; 39 top and bottom; 51; 52 top; 79; Tony Meston pp viii; 8; 26; 28; 57; 100; St Maarten, Saba, and St Eustatius Tourist Office pp 12 top; 14 (photograph Dave Green); 46 (photograph John Forte); 53, 54 (photograph John Forte); 55; 89; 97 (photograph John Forte); 99; 108; 115 (photograph Claire Devener); 116
Cover photograph of Marigot Harbour from Fort Louis courtesy of Michael P. Morrissey

The publishers have made every effort to trace the copyright holders, but if they have inadvertently overlooked any, they will be pleased to make the necessary arrangements at the first opportunity.

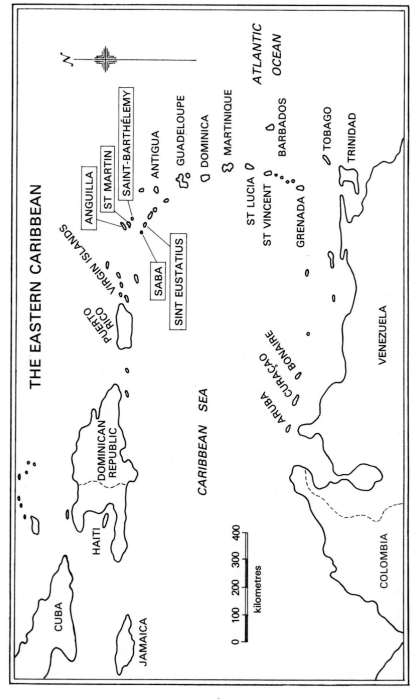

THE EASTERN CARIBBEAN

Preface

The huge crescent of islands called the Lesser Antilles stretches from the Virgin Islands in the north to Aruba in the south, forming the eastern boundary of the Caribbean Sea. From the earliest days of their discovery the islands were divided into two groups — *Las islas de Barlovento* (the islands to the windward) and *Las islas de Sotavento* (the islands to the leeward). These expressions referred to the position of the islands in relation to the prevailing north-easterly trade wind, which brought the original Spanish colonists from Europe. All the islands between the Virgin Islands and Trinidad were 'to windward', and those parallel to the coast of South America were 'to leeward'. These terms were adopted by the French and Dutch settlers but not by the British. For some inexplicable reason all the British possessions between the Virgin Islands and Dominica were called the Leeward Islands, and those to the south as far as Trinidad, the Windward Islands.

Because of the British superiority in the region during the colonial era the latter terms were accepted widely. They have always been the source of much controversy, with mariners and other visitors trying in vain to find a logical geographical reason for the division. That this was an administrative division only is borne out by the fact that in 1940 the island of Dominica was transferred arbitrarily from the Colony of the Leeward Islands to that of the Windward Islands. Although both colonies have long since disappeared and the majority of the islands are now independent states, the terms remain in use locally and still appear on modern British maps and charts.

Some idea of the confusion caused by this prime example of British perversity can be gauged by considering the five Lesser

Philipsburg, between Great Bay and the Great Salt Pond, Sint Maarten

Antillean islands which form the subject of this book. Each is a dependency — using the term in its widest possible connotation — of the Netherlands, France or Great Britain. One island considers itself, and is considered by the British, to be a 'leeward island'. Two and a half islands form the *Bovenwindse Eilanden* (Windward Islands) group of the Netherlands Antilles. The other one and a half islands with true French sang-froid ignore both descriptions. My choice in referring to all of them as 'islands to the windward' is deliberate. The British terms were always confusing, and now that the colonies to which they referred no longer exist they are meaningless.

This inconsistency with regard to a name for the regional grouping is repeated to some extent, but in a different form, in the names of three of the islands. Because one is divided politically it has two names; the Dutch part being called *Sint Maarten* and the French part *Saint-Martin*. I have used the appropriate spelling when referring to one side or the other, but when alluding to the island as a whole I have preferred the Anglicized *St Martin*. *Sint Eustatius* is very often referred to, by the inhabitants and outsiders alike, as *Statia*. *Saint-Barthélemy* is equally widely known by an abbreviated title, variously spelt as *Saint-Barth*, *Saint Barths* or *St Barts*. The other two islands, *Anguilla* and *Saba*, are known by these names and no others.

I am most grateful to the following people for their assistance, and for contributing in all sorts of ways to my understanding of the islands: Cornelius de Weever, Louis Peters and Wallace Peters (St Martin); Elise Magras (Saint-Barthélemy); Alastair Baillie, Bernice Lake, David Carty and Amelia Vanterpool (Anguilla); Neuman Pompier (Sint Eustatius); Will Johnson and Glenn Holm (Saba); Phyllis Mayers, Cuthryn Lake and Violet White (Antigua); and the Director of the Meteorological Service of the Netherlands Antilles (Curaçao). I owe a special word of thanks to Windward Islands Airways for their generous assistance with my travelling between the islands, and to my wife, Veronica, for allowing me to take advantage of it. Any errors of fact or interpretation, and of course all opinions expressed, are solely mine.

Brian Dyde
Antigua
May 1986

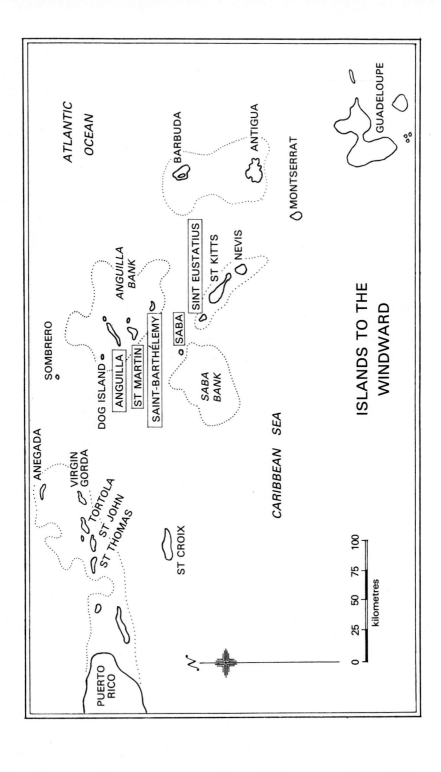

ISLANDS TO THE
WINDWARD

Chapter 1

Five gems of the Caribbean

This book is about five small islands on the rim of the Caribbean Sea, seemingly scattered in no sensible order between the neat grouping of the American and British Virgin Islands to the west, and the independent states of St Christopher and Nevis (more usually known as St Kitts-Nevis) and Antigua and Barbuda to the east. At first glance they have little in common. Three belong to the geological group called the *Limestone Caribbees*, while the other two are of purely volcanic origin. Each is a dependency of one of three European nations. But these differences are far outweighed by those factors they do have in common. Each is very small, ranging from 89 square kilometres to a mere 13 square kilometres in area, and they are all intervisible. They were all settled at about the same time, by much the same sort of people, drawn from many nationalities. Despite frequent changes of ownership their histories are very similar and closely interwoven. Today all five are united in their remoteness from central government, in their dependence and interdependence on tourism, and not least in the widespread use of the English language.

The islands were settled between 1629 and 1650 by people who in the main were poor and oppressed. They were escaping from religious persecution in Europe, from crimes committed at sea and ashore, or from a failure to make a living in the larger islands near by. They were soon joined by assorted castaways, deserters, renegades and other human flotsam of the period. These early settlers had little choice but to make the best of what they found. In every case they found an uninhabited, dry and barren island, with no lakes or permanent streams, little wildlife, and which was subject to the devastations of hurricanes. Those that landed in

1

Saba found, in addition to everything else, that they had to eke out a living from the steep slopes of a mountain which fell on every side precipitously into the sea. To survive these natural disadvantages, as well as all the political turmoil of the next 150 years, they needed to be not only very resilient but also extremely self-sufficient. No wonder then that each island bred people of great character and independent outlook. This marked individuality may have had much to do with the way the white settlers treated the black slaves they soon began to import. Because the islands were so infertile and the land so difficult to work it was not uncommon in Saba and Saint-Barthélemy for whites and blacks to work side by side, and in any of the islands undue harshness on the part of the whites would have been self-defeating. In none of them did the proportion of blacks to whites ever approach the great imbalance found in the neighbouring 'plantation' islands.

Once the islands had been settled, and throughout the remainder of the seventeenth century, they were subjected to constant attacks by marauders of one kind or another — Caribs, pirates and buccaneers — as well as by Spanish forces still attempting to keep other nations out of the Caribbean. This was followed by a century or more of internecine warfare between the French, Dutch and British about their ownership, during which time all but Anguilla changed hands repeatedly. Then for a brief interlude after the end of the Napoleonic wars they were left alone, under the flags of the countries which own them today, to attend to their own affairs, and to try to create viable economies based on agriculture. This did not meet with any great success in any island and was doomed once slavery was abolished. This happened in 1834 in the British colonies, in 1848 in the French ones, and as late as 1863 in the Dutch islands. Once the blacks were free agricultural activity soon became little more than subsistence farming, and dramatic changes took place among the population of each island. In Anguilla, Sint Eustatius and Sint Maarten many of the white proprietors sold out and moved to other countries. In Saba and Saint-Barthélemy the blacks left in large numbers to find work elsewhere.

From the middle of the last century until recent times the islands were of little interest and almost unknown to the outside world, barely recognized even by their Caribbean neighbours. Up until

Grand Case Bay, Saint-Martin

about 1960 they were all underdeveloped, depopulated and depressed, lacking even basic amenities and dependent to a large extent on remittances from their many citizens living overseas. Those who remained made a living from a limited range of occupations — salt-making, fishing, seafaring, boat-building, and subsistence farming.

The occasional visitor to the islands during this period fell into one of a small number of categories. There was the infrequent travel writer, gathering material for a book or magazine article. Many of the books have little that is good to say about either the islands or their inhabitants. One need look no further than the well-known *The Traveller's Tree* by Patrick Leigh Fermor, to see what a talented writer thought of St Martin as it was in the late 1940s. Not all of the magazine articles were so unkind. Even today the visitor to Saba will be shown with pride articles about the island in battered copies of the *National Geographic* published well before the Second World War.

Other visitors included missionaries and yachtsmen. The former were either looking for converts or carrying out an inspection of an existing church organization; the latter were the lonely forerun-

3

ners of the thousands of boat-owners now found in every corner of the Caribbean. From some of the accounts of their visits, it often seems that for the missionary there was not much to differentiate between a journey through the Caribbean islands and one through a remoter part of Africa. At the same time many of the yachtsmen looked upon cruising around the islands with nearly as much trepidation as the early Spanish explorers. A fourth type of visitor was the functionary sent out by the home government to report on some aspect of life in a particular island. Again, from the little material published about such visits, the impression gained is that most officials looked upon them as something to be endured and completed as quickly as possible. Few visitors had anything good to say about the islands, and their books, reports and articles contain many disparaging remarks.

Such remarks, it has to be admitted, had much foundation in fact, as can be seen from a few observations about the islands. Communications with the outside world were very poor; so much so in the case of Saint-Barthélemy that news of the ending of the First World War was not received until nearly two weeks after the signing of the Armistice. All the islands were badly surveyed and mapped until well into the twentieth century; both Saint-Martin and Saint-Barthélemy were unsurveyed until 1949, and the only maps until then were sketch maps drawn by local residents. The first motor vehicle was landed on Saba in 1947, and up until 1963 the only way of reaching the island was to be rowed ashore through the surf. Sint Eustatius was without any banking facilities until 1969. None of the islands had public electricity or water supplies until well on into the 1960s. Even today Anguilla, Saint-Martin and Sint Eustatius have only rudimentary port facilities. Nearly every public service and basic amenity has been acquired only within the last 25 years. Probably the single greatest spur to their provision has been the growth of tourism over the same period.

Tourism came first to Sint Maarten, where the first beach hotel was opened in 1955, and then had an effect on each of the other islands in turn. The overall result has been profound and all of them have been transformed to a greater or lesser extent. None now bears any resemblance to its moribund former self. Tourism, despite the well-known drawbacks attached to its dominance of an

The beautiful white sand beach at Maho Bay, Sint Maarten

island's economy, has become all-important to each of them. It has also forced the inhabitants of each island to carry out a reappraisal of their island's attributes and to review their relationship with the outside world. The three northern islands — Anguilla, St Martin and Saint-Barthélemy — all fit into the classic image of the tourist resort. All three today give the impression of being in a state of transition, as if their inhabitants have decided to transform them by getting rid of as much of the past as possible. In contrast, Saba and Sint Eustatius both retain a distinct air of changelessness, their inhabitants realizing perhaps that their future relies on retaining the closest possible links with the past.

Regardless of this broad division into two groups each island is a very individual, identifiable place, offering its own special attractions to the visitor. St Martin has a distinct cosmopolitan air; Saint-Barthélemy possesses a chic French atmosphere with North American overtones; Sint Eustatius preserves a sense of history and past glory; Anguilla retains a distinctly Anglicized way of life; and Saba — well, Saba is just unlike *any* other island. Between them they offer everything the visitor to the Caribbean could want, whether it is scenery, sights, history, water-sports, beaches, trekking, shopping bargains, *haute cuisine*, a naturist resort, gambling, or merely a totally relaxed vacation in guaranteed sunshine. Any or all of these can be obtained with no greater effort than choosing an itinerary and making the necessary travel arrangements. For the visitor who still needs something more — who would like to discover the *real* islands — a little more effort is required.

Even though each island is small this should not lead anyone to think that the inhabitants are equally small-minded or provincial. In Sint Maarten, where the population has increased during the past 25 years from less than 1500 to over 20 000 (such has been the speed of the increase that no one knows the exact figure), it is very likely that the majority of the people are much more widely travelled than most of the tourists who visit each year. Even in tiny Saba, with its 1000 or so people, a sizeable number of them were born in places as far apart as England and Colombia, Haiti and Surinam. It is the islanders who have made the islands what they are today. No one from outside can fully appreciate Sint Maarten, Saba, or any of the other islands without taking into account the diverse experiences, the hardships and the long years of exile that have gone into creating the modern society and way of life.

In each island most of the inhabitants the visitor will come into contact with will be connected in some way or other with the tourist industry. In true small-island fashion, undoubtedly all will be courteous, helpful and friendly. But, as in any other place dependent on tourism, such contacts are likely to be superficial and restricted to the business in hand, whether this is serving a drink, wrapping a gift or conducting a sight-seeing tour. This superficiality might well be termed the 'tourist industry façade'. By making an effort to penetrate this, to get to know individuals — whether they are part of the 'industry' or not — even the most transitory visitor will be rewarded.

At first sight a small island with a limited number of either natural or man-made attractions will have, for many visitors, an equally limited appeal. Genuine, friendly contact with even just

Making friends

one or two local people will open up whole new aspects. It would not be going too far to say that, except for the confirmed recluse or completely unsociable, the pleasure of a visit to any of these islands will increase in direct proportion to the number of acquaintances and friends made amongst the inhabitants. This book is not intended as a primer in how to go about this. Rather it is intended as an introduction, which it is hoped will prompt readers to continue their own discoveries of what I for one consider to be five priceless gems of the Caribbean.

Chapter 2

More about the islands

Location and formation

Some 560 km to the east of the island of Hispaniola, and 800 km north of Venezuela, is a large bank of shallow water separating the Caribbean Sea from the Atlantic Ocean. In the distant past the Anguilla Bank was probably one large island. Today only about

The windward coast of St Martin

five per cent of it appears above water — in the shape of the islands of Anguilla, St Martin and Saint-Barthélemy — together with the many small islets and rocks which surround them. To the south, and separated from the Anguilla Bank by about 24 km of very deep water, is another bank with three islands. This bank has no name but the islands are Nevis, St Kitts and, at the north-western end, Sint Eustatius. Yet a third bank, the shallowest of them all, is found about 20 km to the west of Sint Eustatius. This is called the Saba Bank. No islands or rocks appear above its surface. The island of Saba is not on the bank, but rises out of deep water close to the north-eastern side.

Anguilla, St Martin and Saint-Barthélemy belong to the outer arc of the eastern Caribbean islands, frequently referred to as the *Limestone Caribbees*. These are the fairly low islands which were created by the raising of coral reefs above the sea during the periods of intense geological and volcanic activity which took place perhaps 35 million years ago. Anguilla is the northernmost of these islands, which begin at Barbados in the south. On the Caribbean side of these islands, and roughly parallel to them, is another chain of islands, all mountainous and all created by volcanic action. Saba and Sint Eustatius are at the northern end of this chain, and are very different in appearance from their three neighbours to the north. The limestone islands have very irregular coastlines and fine white sand beaches, while the two volcanic islands have far fewer bays with beaches made of coarse black sand.

Climate

Because of their position within the tropics all the islands have high average air temperatures throughout the year. In Sint Maarten, where meteorological records have been kept for many years, and where conditions do not differ significantly from those in any of the others, the mean temperature ranges from 25 °C in January to 28 °C in August. The relative humidity varies from around 68 per cent in the spring to 74 per cent in the autumn. Any adverse effect from the combination of high temperature and a fairly high humidity is more than offset by the constancy with which the islands are cooled by the trade wind. This blows from a direction between north-east and south-east for about 300 days of the year, usually at between 10 and 15 knots. Any difference in the climate between the five islands stems from their relative sizes and elevations, and the effect the presence of hills and mountains has on rainfall. Saba, being the most mountainous, has far more cloud than the others and this reduces the amount of sunshine while increasing the rainfall. Because of this Saba has an average rainfall of about 1140 mm a year, compared with between 900 mm and 1060 mm in the other islands. These figures are averages obtained over a long period; the rainfall in all of them is erratic, varying widely from year to year as well as from month to month. Taking long-term averages the year is divided into a 'dry' season from December to July, when the average monthly rainfall may be as low as 12 mm, and a 'wet' season from August to November when — in a good year — the monthly average may be as much as 300 mm. In the short-term though, the only sure thing about rainfall is that any month may be 'wet' or 'dry'.

The only time when these highly agreeable conditions are likely to change significantly is between July and November in the 'hurricane season'. Along with all the other Caribbean islands these five are equally at risk from the effects of a tropical storm. These effects are well known and need no elaboration here. In the

Great Bay, Sint Maarten

islands adequate warning systems operate, and sound precautions are taken to protect life and property. While to visit one of the islands during this season, particularly in August or September, will involve the risk of seeing the effect of a hurricane at firsthand, the chances of doing so are fairly small.

Attempts have been made in textbooks and learned papers to fit the climate of these islands into some world-wide classification system. It has been described variously as 'belonging to the tropical summer rainfall zone', as a 'tropical climate with seasonal rainfall', and as 'intermediate between one with a marked dry season and one with an intense dry season'. None of these descriptions is adequate. For most of the year the sun shines, the temperature of both the air and the sea are high (and within a couple of degrees of each other), a cooling breeze blows steadily, and rain falls in infrequent brief showers — in short it is perfect vacation weather. A much more meaningful climatic description would be 'the tourist ideal', producing conditions which enhance life and health, and encourage relaxation.

Plants

At the time of their discovery by the Spanish in the fifteenth century each island was covered with some kind of forest. This was quickly reduced in size as they were settled and agricultural activity started. Today the only areas of genuine forest left are on the upper slopes of Mount Scenery in Saba, and inside the crater of the extinct volcano called The Quill in Sint Eustatius. Much of St Martin is covered by thorn scrub and coarse grassland, which in the tropics soon takes over land which is allowed to lie idle or has been over-grazed. During periods of rainfall the island takes on a very pleasant green appearance from a distance, but in drier times it soon becomes brown and parched-looking. This is very much the picture in Anguilla, Saint-Barthélemy and Sint Eustatius; only Saba is different. This island, in comparison with the others, is luxuriant with trees and other vegetation. The structure of Saba has never permitted anything other than the making of tiny fields on some of the lesser slopes, and over-grazing has never been a problem. The amount of vegetation increases

Vegetation with richly coloured flowers is characteristic of Saba

Anguillan house and garden

with altitude until, at about 500 m, the whole of the top of Mount Scenery is covered with a genuine tropical rain forest. Similar growth — tall trees with lots of verdant undergrowth, lianas, ferns and mosses — exists inside The Quill on Sint Eustatius.

Common tropical shrubs such as the hibiscus and oleander, and flowering trees like the poinciana and frangipani, grow well in all the islands. They do much to offset the bland green (or more usual brown) hills. The majority are cultivated as ornamental plants, and their brightly coloured flowers add much to the appearance of even the most undistinguished garden or forecourt. Where they are grown around buildings of true character — be this an old house on Saba, a well-designed modern hotel in Anguilla, or a luxurious residence in Saint-Barthélemy — the overall effect is extremely picturesque.

Animals and birds

While all the islands at one time had much more vegetation than they do today, it is improbable that their wildlife was ever much more extensive than at present. In each island it consists of little more than rats, mice, bats and lizards with a few iguanas. St Martin also has mongooses, which were introduced in the last century. A few snakes are found on Anguilla, and on the higher ground of both Saba and Sint Eustatius. Probably bats are the most diverse and widespread species of mammal, and there are many in every island, living on fruit and insects.

The bird life is rather more varied, but still limited in species and overall numbers. Just over fifty different kinds of bird have been recorded in St Martin, with between thirty and forty in all the other islands. Of these many are migratory species from North America. The commonest birds are hummingbirds, bananaquits, ground doves and pearly-eyed thrashers. Because of their mountains Saba and Sint Eustatius are the homes of one or two species not found in the northern islands. The red-tailed buzzard and the lesser Antillean kestrel can be seen on Saba, while The Quill is the habitat of tremblers and a few rare blue pigeons. In the other islands their salt ponds provide good habitats for herons, egrets, ducks and waders, particularly during the migratory season. There are seven or eight sea-birds which are common throughout the area, breeding on the cliffs or on the various rocks and islets of the Anguilla Bank. Besides the unmistakable brown pelican they include sooty terns, brown noddys, shearwaters, brown boobies and the red-billed tropicbird. Sea-birds will form the majority of the birds seen by the average visitor, after the ubiquitous bananaquits and bullfinches seen around any outside dining area.

Marine life

The life in the sea around them is much more varied than that on the islands themselves. There are large areas of coral reef along the shores of Anguilla, St Martin and Saint-Barthélemy which support large numbers of fish, shellfish, lobsters and sea-urchins. Fishing on the Anguilla Bank and the Saba Bank has been an occupation

Colourful fish in the sea off Sint Eustatius

for generations of islanders, and the species caught include tunny, mackerel, snapper, dolphin and swordfish. Fishing for a living has declined greatly in recent years. This has nothing to do with a decline in the fish population, but much to do with the more attractive and less arduous occupations now available ashore. The waters around the islands offer plenty of excitement to the keen

Marigot, Saint-Martin

sport fisherman, just as the inshore reefs provide excellent oppor-
tunities for snorkelling, scuba-diving and spear-fishing.

Sea turtles feed around the coasts of all the islands. Some of the
beaches of Anguilla, St Martin and Saint-Barthélemy are used as
nesting areas during the breeding season from June to September.
The most common variety is the hawksbill, but the green turtle is
also seen from time to time. Other kinds, such as the loggerhead or
the leatherback (which is the largest of the species), may also be
encountered now and then by fishermen and divers. There are
well run diving centres of one kind or another in each island.
Those in Saba and Sint Eustatius offer courses geared to the
requirements of the professional diving enthusiast. The waters
around these two islands, which are more or less free from coral
reefs, are exceptionally clear. The underwater rock formations and
plant life are of considerable interest to divers, photographers and
marine biologists alike.

Chapter 3

More about the people

All five islands are linked by common historical and economic factors. At the same time they are divided geologically into two groups. From this point of view the three islands on the Anguilla Bank have very little in common with the two volcanic islands to the south. The islands may also be divided on the basis of their administration.

The administration of the Dutch islands

The three *Bovenwindse Eilanden* were initially administered by the Dutch West India Company, when they were not occupied by the British or French. After the end of the wars of the eighteenth century the islands were administered for a time by a Governor-General and his political council at Paramaribo in Surinam. This lasted until 1845 when the islands became dependencies of the newly-formed colony of Curaçao, which had a Governor who was responsible to the Colonial Office of the Netherlands. Each island had a Lieutenant-Governor appointed from Curaçao, with two local counsellors to advise him on matters such as the budget, schools and public services. In 1922, under the Netherlands Constitution Act, Curaçao became an integral part of the Kingdom of the Netherlands, and so at one remove did each of the three Windward Islands.

In 1936 a legislative body called the *Staten* was formed in Curaçao. This had fifteen members, five of whom were appointed by the Governor and the other ten elected by limited suffrage (at the time about five per cent of the population). The Windward

The Court House at Philipsburg, Sint Maarten

Islands elected one member between them. This rather unsatisfactory state of affairs lasted until 1948 when full adult suffrage was introduced. For six years of this period the Netherlands Antilles had to administer themselves in isolation, as the motherland was in enemy hands. After that experience it was only a matter of time before they were granted full autonomy in their internal affairs, and this took place in 1954. In that year the *Staten* was enlarged to 22 members and given full legislative authority. The Windward Islands continued to elect only one member, and this inevitably was someone from Sint Maarten.

They were now administered by a Lieutenant-Governor in Sint Maarten, assisted by an Administrator in each of the other islands. All three had elected councils with complete autonomy in purely local affairs. The members of these councils met from time to time in Sint Maarten to form what was known as the Island Council, to discuss matters of mutual interest. In 1983 the Administrators of Saba and Sint Eustatius were replaced by Lieutenant-Governors. Each island now administers its own affairs with the Lieutenant-Governor being assisted by two Commissioners; these Commissioners are elected from among those members of the party which holds the most seats in the island's council.

On 1 January 1986 the island of Aruba left the Netherlands Antilles to become a completely independent country 'in association' with the Netherlands. The events leading up to this caused the administration of the remaining islands to be reviewed and revised once again. Towards the end of 1985 the composition of the *Staten* was amended, and elections were held for new representatives, now called senators. For the first time Sint Eustatius and Saba were each given a seat, and Sint Maarten's representation was increased to three seats. At the same time each island adopted an individual national flag and a coat of arms. It is of course still too early to see what advantages the new administrative set-up will provide for the Windward Islands, but at least each island now has its own voice in the *Staten*, with perhaps a greater sense of national identity and self-awareness.

The administration of the French islands

With the end of the Napoleonic era in 1815 the French possessions in the Caribbean became Crown Colonies. Saint-Martin, as a dependency of a much larger island, was administered by a military commander responsible to the Governor of Guadeloupe. In 1838 the military commander was replaced by a civilian mayor. From 1882 the mayor and the members of the Municipal Council were elected by universal suffrage. Saint-Barthélemy, which had belonged to Sweden for almost a hundred years, was returned to French rule in 1878. It too was made a dependency of Guadeloupe with an elected mayor and council.

During the Third Republic from 1871 to 1940 French colonial policy was one of 'assimilation' for all overseas possessions. The West Indian islands were given representation in the French Assembly in Paris, and the inhabitants granted equal rights with those of the people of France. 'Assimilation' was not universally successful, but did achieve its aim in the Caribbean. After the Second World War Guadeloupe became an overseas *département* with the same constitutional position as a metropolitan department. The Governor was replaced by a Prefect, appointed from Paris, and a *Conseil Général* was elected with members from both Saint-Martin and Saint-Barthélemy. Each island became a *commune* of the *arrondissement* of Basse-Terre, which is one of the three subdivisions of Guadeloupe. The two islands are administered by a *Sous-préfet* who lives in Saint-Martin. This official is appointed from Paris and is the equivalent of the Lieutenant-Governor in one of the Dutch islands. The day-to-day running of each island is still carried out by an elected mayor and the *Conseil Municipal*.

This form of administration, evolved and modified over the past 40 years, has enabled both islands to profit from being considered part of France. They each receive a fair share of direct assistance

French colonial architecture, Marigot, Saint-Martin

with public expenditure, the protection of the French police and military authorities, and the benefits of membership of the European Economic Community. While still closely linked with Guadeloupe they have escaped from being just small colonial outposts of the larger island with no direct contact with central government.

The administration of Anguilla

Anguilla was not so fortunate. From 1882 the island was part of the then Presidency and later Colony of St Christopher, Nevis and Anguilla. This unification was carried out without considering the wishes of the Anguillan population, and with no purpose other than to create a tidy colonial administration operating for the benefit of the British Government. When the colony was granted independence 'in association' with Great Britain in 1967 Anguilla was left with no direct recourse to the British Government, and under the rule of an unsympathetic, if not hostile, administration in St Kitts. A series of events (which are discussed in more detail in Chapter 7) in the following years led to the reinstatement of a British Commissioner, the granting of a separate constitution, formal separation from St Kitts and Nevis, and finally in 1982 to the recognition of Anguilla as once again a dependent territory of the United Kingdom.

The island is now administered by a Governor who is appointed by, and directly responsible to, the British Foreign and Commonwealth Office in London. He is assisted by an Executive Council, consisting of himself, four Ministers of Government, the Attorney-General and the Permanent Secretary (Finance). The House of Assembly is composed of seven elected members (from whom the Ministers are drawn), two members nominated by the Governor, two official members — the Attorney-General and the Permanent Secretary (Finance) — and a Speaker through whom all the business of the House is conducted. The Governor has responsibility for all external affairs, defence and internal security, as well as the administration of the Public Service. Responsibility for all other matters is delegated to the Chief Minister, who apportions this responsibility between himself and his three

21

ministerial colleagues. The island, to all intents and purposes, is internally self-governing.

Despite the differences in outward appearances and in the titles and forms of address used among the various representatives of the people, the administration of all five islands is very similar. None is responsible for its own defence or diplomatic relations with the outside world, but each has more or less full control over its internal affairs and the welfare of its inhabitants. Considering the size of each island and its total resources this is probably not an unenviable situation. It is certainly a situation which seems to satisfy the vast majority of the population in all of them. The events of the late 1960s in Anguilla forced the British Government into taking far more interest in the island. Because of some less traumatic episodes in the French Caribbean in recent years there is no doubt that the French Government is now paying more attention to its Caribbean *départements*. With the very recent change in the structure of the Netherlands Antilles, which has enabled the Windward Islands to take on more individual identities along with their new flags and national anthems, the attention of the Dutch Government too has been drawn to the region. Strenuous efforts are being made in each island to develop and strengthen the economy, but to undertake any major development project not connected directly with the tourist industry requires the involvement of central government. In this respect the current revival of interest in The Hague, Paris and London in what is happening among their Caribbean possessions must be of benefit to each of these five islands.

Languages

Another factor which might be expected to divide the islands, considering their long association with three European countries, is language. Dutch is the official language of Sint Maarten, Sint Eustatius and Saba, and French of Saint-Martin and Saint-Barthélemy, while English is the language of Anguilla. However, the visitor to any of the Dutch islands is unlikely to hear any

Dutch being spoken, or to see anything written in that language other than signs on official buildings or in official documents. The strange 'foreign' language which may be heard occasionally in Sint Maarten is *Papiamento*. This is the only new language ever to be developed in the Caribbean region. It originated in the three islands of the Netherlands Antilles off the coast of Venezuela: Curaçao, Bonaire and Aruba, and is derived from Spanish, Portuguese, English and Dutch with African and Amerindian elements. It was never used in the Windward Islands until recent years, but has been brought back by the thousands of people who went to the southern islands to find work and who have now returned home. For those who do not speak *Papiamento*, English is their first language with Dutch a poor second.

In Saint-Martin, while French is used far more extensively than is Dutch in Sint Maarten, English is the language used by most people. In Saint-Barthélemy the reverse is true; French is *the* language and the use of English is more restricted. The Creole patois which is used widely in the larger French islands is not heard to any great extent either in Saint-Martin or in Saint-Barthélemy. The unwary visitor to Anguilla might well imagine, from overhearing a local conversation, that Anguillans also speak some sort of patois. This is far from being so; English is the one and only language, but Anguillans, like the inhabitants of all the other ex-British West Indian islands, have developed their own dialect. Its use is generally restricted to private conversations within certain sections of the community, and it is dropped when talking to outsiders.

Although determined efforts are being made by the authorities to preserve the use of French and Dutch it is not too hard to imagine, within this group of islands, these languages becoming the Caribbean equivalents of mandarin with their use restricted to fewer and fewer officials as time goes by. Throughout all five islands English is the lingua franca and with their future so heavily dependent on tourism it is difficult to see this trend towards a common language being reversed. While this may not do much for the blood pressures of the 'Immortals' of the Académie française, or their Dutch equivalents, it surely has a great deal to do with the ever-increasing popularity of the islands for the North American tourists who form the great majority of their visitors.

In the previous chapter it was suggested that the climate of the islands could well be termed the 'tourist ideal'. Here I have tried to show that the present administration of all five has much merit. Each is secure and stable, with the inhabitants exercising full and mature responsibility for their own internal well-being while leaving their external interests in more powerful hands. Even if the islanders themselves, given their stubborn independent characters, would never admit to this being a situation as ideal as the climate they enjoy, it certainly would be thought so in many other parts of the wider Caribbean region. Similarly, the way the islands are organized to receive visitors and the arrangements which exist for travelling between them are equally impressive, and could well be emulated elsewhere in the region.

Chapter 4

Travelling to and between the islands

Travelling by air

St Martin is central to the group both geographically and economically. The number of visitors it receives each year far exceeds the total received by all four of the other islands put together. The majority of these visitors arrive by air at the **Juliana International Airport** in Sint Maarten, and this airport is fundamental to all air travel between the islands. Each of the other islands has its own airport and these, with the exception of that on Saba, all have connections with islands outside the group, although the main air traffic is to and from Sint Maarten.

Juliana International Airport, Sint Maarten

Juliana Airport handles over 100 aircraft movements a day and more than three-quarters of a million passengers each year. There are scheduled flights to and from Europe, North America and South America, as well as numerous other Caribbean islands. Since the original airstrip was constructed during the Second World War the airport facilities have been rebuilt and extended on several occasions. The single runway can now handle large wide-bodied jets as well as the Concorde, and the present terminal buildings were opened in 1985. There is a small airfield in Saint-Martin, called **Espérance**, which was opened in 1973. It is used for purely local traffic to Saint-Barthélemy, Guadeloupe and Anguilla. Considering that it is no more than 15 km from Juliana Airport, its construction — involving the reclamation of part of a salt pond — must be seen as little more than a symbolic gesture on behalf of the French authorities.

The airports in Anguilla, Saint-Barthélemy, Saba and Sint Eustatius handle scheduled daily flights to and from Sint Maarten, together with less frequent flights from some of them to the neighbouring islands of Antigua, St Kitts, the Virgin Islands and Puerto Rico. For reasons which will become apparent later the airport on Saba is restricted to use by aircraft belonging to *Windward Islands Airways*, connecting the island with Sint Maarten and Sint Eustatius only. The time taken to travel between any of the islands is very small, ranging from 10 minutes between Sint Maarten and Saint-Barthélemy to perhaps 20

Grand Case Bay and Espérance Airport

Coming in to land, Saint-Barthélemy

minutes from Sint Maarten to Sint Eustatius. The inter-island flights are so arranged that it is easy and convenient to visit any of the others from Sint Maarten on a daily basis, leaving in the early morning and returning before nightfall. The return in the early evening is necessary as none of the smaller airfields, other than that in Anguilla, is equipped for night flying.

Travelling by sea

Most visitors arriving in St Martin by sea do so in one of the many Caribbean cruise ships, staying for perhaps 10 or 12 hours. These ships either anchor in the entrance to Great Bay, on the south coast of Sint Maarten, or berth on the pier on the eastern side of the bay near Point Blanche. The cruise ship traffic, which started in the late 1950s, has grown to over 200 ship-calls a year. There are often two or three such vessels in Great Bay at the same time during the most popular cruising months. Passengers from those at anchor are landed at a small pier in the centre of the waterfront of Philipsburg, which lines the head of Great Bay. Saint-Barthélemy and Saba each have a much smaller number of regular cruise ship visits, and Sint Eustatius has the odd call by some of the smaller vessels. Anguilla has yet to be discovered by the cruise ship operators.

The next most popular method of arriving by sea in any of the islands is in a yacht. All five islands are of interest to yachtsmen, but only the waters around the three on the Anguilla Bank provide a reasonable cruising ground. Out of these three only St Martin has all the facilities required in the way of boat-yards, chandleries, marinas and protected moorings, and these are concentrated in Great Bay and in Simpson Bay Lagoon. Saint-Barthélemy is the next most popular island for yachtsmen, and Gustavia Harbour becomes very crowded with boats at anchor during the winter months. Anguilla has some excellent and safe anchorages but very limited shoreside facilities. Saba and Sint Eustatius can provide nothing in the way of facilities and only one or two poor anchorages. This is not to say that the two southern islands are seldom visited by yachtsmen since both are too attractive to be bypassed during a serious Caribbean cruise. However, yacht visits to either are governed very much by the weather and sea conditions, and are likely for that reason to be much briefer than to any of the other islands. For the yachtsman who does not have unlimited time during which to wait for the right sea conditions, probably the easiest way of visiting Saba or Sint Eustatius is to leave his boat in a marina in Sint Maarten and to complete the journey by air.

Gustavia Harbour, Saint-Barthélemy

The ferry to Anguilla from Marigot, Saint-Martin

It is possible to reach the islands by sea in something other than a large liner or a yacht. There are plenty of small coasters and schooners which trade between this group and other islands in the region. Not many of these will carry passengers as a matter of course, but the persistent traveller with time to spare normally will be able to find a berth. Standards of comfort and hygiene may well leave much to be desired but any discomfort is bound to be outweighed by the value of the experience.

Anchorage at St Martin

Travel by sea within the group is reasonably well organized but limited. There is a regular and expanding ferry service, with scheduled departure and arrival times, between Blowing Point Harbour in Anguilla and Marigot, the capital of Saint-Martin. During the main tourist season what amounts to a daily ferry service between Sint Maarten and Saint-Barthélemy is operated by a number of large yachts, working out of a marina in Great Bay. As all of them offer a day in Saint-Barthélemy with free drinks there and back, at a fare slightly less than the return air fare, they provide an excellent alternative method of transport between the two islands. It is also possible to travel by yacht from Sint Maarten to Saba or Sint Eustatius, but such trips are made on an irregular basis as the demand arises.

Arrival in the islands

Regardless of the means of transportation used to reach the islands the arrival formalities are simple and straightforward. They are particularly so in St Martin and Saint-Barthélemy on account of their duty-free status, there being no customs procedure of any kind. Saba and Sint Eustatius are also duty-free — by default because of their close relationship with Sint Maarten — from where nearly everything they import as well as nearly all their visitors are transferred. Anguilla, however, is *not* duty-free and visitors, perhaps made over-complacent by the freedom of travel between the other four islands, must be prepared for the more usual regulations about duty-free allowances and possible baggage inspection.

The entry regulations between the Dutch, French and British islands differ slightly. For Sint Maarten, Saba and Sint Eustatius a valid passport and an onward or return ticket are all that are required from any visitor. In Saint-Martin and Saint-Barthélemy the same requirements exist for anyone from the USA, Canada, Great Britain or Sweden; for visitors from any other country the regulations are the same as those which apply in France, and a visa may well be needed. In Anguilla most visitors will require nothing more than a passport and return ticket, but a visa may be needed by citizens of certain countries outside North America and the

British Commonwealth. Regardless of which island is being visited the entry procedure is conducted in a very friendly and relaxed manner. All visitors intending to stay for more than a day are required to provide an intended address. If this is not known it can cause some delay in gaining entry.

Accommodation

Each island has a sufficiently large range of accommodation to meet the peak demand, and it is being increased everywhere to keep up with the steadily rising number of visitors expected each year. Accommodation is available in everything from a 600-room resort on St Martin to a one-room 'efficiency apartment' on Saba, with every conceivable type of hotel, guest-house, villa or cottage in between. Each island has its own well-organized and efficient Tourist Department which can supply all the necessary details you will need.

Sint Maarten	The Tourist Bureau
	De Ruyterplein
	Philipsburg
	Sint Maarten
	Tel: 2337
Saint-Martin	The Visitors' Bureau
	Mairie de Marigot
	Rue Charles de Gaulle
	Marigot
	Saint-Martin
	Tel: 87 50 04
Saint-Barthélemy	Office Municipal de Tourisme
	Rue August Nyman
	Gustavia
	Saint-Barthélemy
	Tel: 27 60 08
Anguilla	The Department of Tourism
	The Valley
	Anguilla
	Tel: 2451

31

Sint Eustatius	The Tourist Office
	Oranjestad
	Sint Eustatius
	Tel: 2225
Saba	Saba Tourist Bureau
	Windwardside
	Saba
	Tel: 2231

The Tourist Bureau in Sint Maarten is the one which has been established the longest, and has by far the largest clientele. It is extremely well run and, together with the equally competent Chamber of Commerce, it publishes or promotes a very wide range of literature to do with tourism in St Martin generally. The Tourist Department in each of the other islands produces written information of varying standards and usefulness. The one item of printed information which is seemingly unobtainable in all the islands, with the exception of Anguilla, is a large scale topographical map. Such maps of the Dutch islands have not been available, to my knowledge, since at least 1982; the situation in the French islands is not much better. The over-simplified sketch maps and black and white, over-reduced reproductions of the genuine articles which are available leave a great deal to be desired. While these probably provide as much information as is needed by most visitors, anyone wanting to explore the islands properly will find them very inadequate. On the other hand, the absence of a proper map of, say, Sint Eustatius means that the visitor intent on seeing as much of the island as possible will have to seek local information and guidance, and such human contacts undoubtedly will prove more rewarding than the study of what, after all, is only a sheet of paper.

Currencies

In the Dutch islands the official currency is the Netherlands Antilles guilder or florin (NAf). This does not have the same value as the Dutch florin, but is tied to the US dollar at the rate of NAf 1.77 to US$ 1.00. This rate varies slightly if the latter is used in stores or restaurants. In the French islands the currency is of course the French franc, and the exchange rate with the US dollar varies in accordance with the international market fluctuations. Anguilla uses the Eastern Caribbean (EC) dollar. This also is tied to the US dollar, but at the rate of EC\$ 2.70 to US\$ 1.00. Everywhere, as may be expected, the US dollar is used almost exclusively. Hotel rates in all the islands are quoted in this currency, as are the prices in many stores, particularly in Sint Maarten. The usual traveller's cheques and credit cards are accepted everywhere in St Martin and Saint-Barthélemy, but there is limited scope for their use in the other islands.

Dress and behaviour

One of the many attractions of the islands is the delightful air of informality which pervades nearly every aspect of life. This is apparent from the moment of arrival, which for nine out of ten visitors will be at Juliana Airport. There is an almost complete absence of uniforms outside the airports in St Martin or any of the other islands. The police force in each is minute and inconspicuous; customs officials exist only in Anguilla and there is no military establishment anywhere. Even the little uniformed officialdom which does exist has its own distinctively West Indian appearance and attitudes. The female airport security guard who can wear her uniform, complete with belt, badges, truncheon, whistle and lanyard, together with elegant high-heeled shoes, two-inch drop ear-rings, and long, painted fingernails says much for the relaxed and tolerant way of life found in all the islands.

This degree of informality extends to visitors and how they are expected to dress and behave. The casual style of dressing is fully acceptable — ties and jackets for men and formal dresses for women are not required — but this should not be taken to extremes. Bathing suits, abbreviated shorts and see-through clothing are *not* acceptable in public places. The islanders are naturally polite and modest, and expect visitors to be the same. Shouting, jostling and displays of anger in public are deprecated as much as unsuitable clothing and ostentation. This view extends from the formal dining table to the beach. While topless bathing is acceptable on some beaches in Saint-Martin (where indeed there is at least one naturist resort) and Saint-Barthélemy, it is not so acceptable in Sint Maarten, and is definitely unacceptable in Anguilla. In Saba and Sint Eustatius the absence of proper beaches makes it unlikely that anyone has given the matter much thought. In general, those visitors who make the effort to conform to the local values of behaviour and dress will risk no embarrassment and probably add to the enjoyment of their stay.

Chapter 5

The shared island — St Martin

St Martin is the only island in the Caribbean other than Hispaniola which is divided politically. Anyone visiting the much larger island, which is shared between Haiti and the Dominican Republic, will have no difficulty from the moment of arrival in recognizing which country is being visited. The same cannot be said for the visitor to St Martin. The division between the southern Dutch part and the northern French part makes no difference to travel from one side of the border to the other. The only indication of the existence of an international frontier is a small monument beside the road which joins Philipsburg and Marigot. English is spoken throughout the island and the majority of signs are in that language. Regardless of nationality, the inhabitants live and work on either side of the border. It is hardly surprising in these circumstances that the visitor sees only one country, and finds the political division of little relevance. In this context it seems sensible therefore to deal with St Martin as a whole, looking at its character, history, development and attractions as an island, and not as two separate countries.

The island

The island is some 900 km to the north-east of Curaçao, the seat of government of the Netherlands Antilles, and about 240 km north-west of Guadeloupe. It is roughly triangular in shape and about 89 square kilometres in size. Saint-Martin occupies the larger portion of about 52 square kilometres, and Sint Maarten the remaining 37 square kilometres. The western corner is low and flat and mostly

35

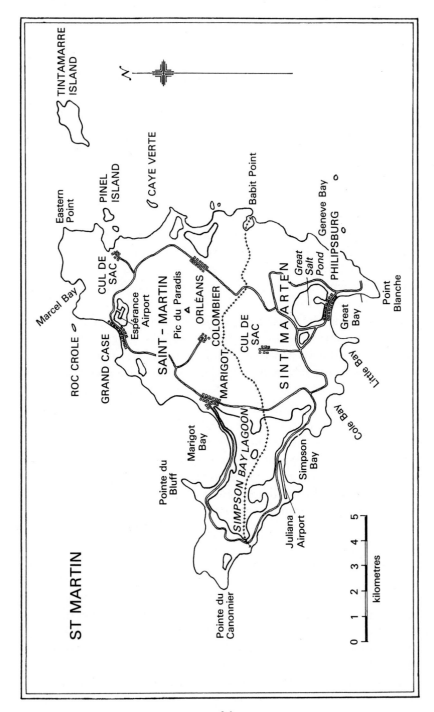

ST MARTIN

TINTAMARRE ISLAND

Eastern Point

PINEL ISLAND

CAYE VERTE

Marcel Bay

CUL DE SAC

ROC CROLE

GRAND CASE

Espérance Airport

SAINT – MARTIN

Pic du Paradis

ORLÉANS

COLOMBIER

MARIGOT

CUL DE SAC

Babit Point

Great Salt Pond

Geneve Bay

PHILIPSBURG

SINT MAARTEN

Point Blanche

Great Bay

Little Bay

Cole Bay

Pointe du Bluff

Marigot Bay

SIMPSON BAY LAGOON

Simpson Bay

Juliana Airport

Pointe du Canonnier

0   1   2   3   4   5
kilometres

taken up by a large lake called **Simpson Bay Lagoon**. This lake is separated by narrow strips of land from Simpson Bay in the south and Marigot Bay in the north. It is deep enough to accommodate boats and yachts, and is used extensively as a safe anchorage for small craft of all kinds. The main entrance is at the eastern end of Simpson Bay. The remainder of the island is hilly except for an area called **Belle Plaine** on the east coast. The main range of hills runs through the middle of the island from **Cole Bay** on the south coast to **Eastern Point**, which is the north-eastern extremity. The highest point of this range, **Pic du Paradis** (424 m), is also the highest point on the island. Belle Plaine is between these hills and a smaller, lower range which runs along the south-east coast.

The whole coastline is indented with bays, all with magnificent white sand beaches. Behind many of them are extensive salt ponds, shallow lakes of brackish water or swamps. Close offshore along the east coast there are several small islets. The largest, **Tintamarre**, is about 4 km off Eastern Point. This is the only one ever to have been inhabited, but it has been deserted since about 1950. Tintamarre is covered with scrub, and this same sort of tough low vegetation covers all the hills of St Martin. Belle Plaine and the much smaller valleys running into the main range of hills are mostly grassland with a few tall trees here and there. When viewed from the sea, especially after periods of heavy rain, the island appears to be very green and heavily wooded.

Discovery and the first settlers

St Martin is popularly supposed to have been discovered by Columbus during his second voyage to the New World in 1493. This is undoubtedly not true. The great explorer did name one of the islands he sighted on that voyage after St Martin of Tours, but this is now known to have been the present island of Nevis. From the most credible reconstruction of the route he took through this part of the Caribbean it is virtually impossible that he could have sighted the present St Martin. The transposition of the name came about at a later date when subsequent Spanish explorers discovered more islands to the north of those found by Columbus, and attempted to identify these on the maps produced from the

1493 expedition. At the time when the island was first sighted by a European it had long been known to and occupied by Amerindians. Evidence of their occupation has been found, particularly around the shores of Simpson Bay Lagoon, but the island had no permanent habitation when the Spanish landed. The Carib name for it, according to a popular history of the island, was *Sualouiga*, although it is recorded elsewhere as 'Sualougia' or 'Oualachi', supposedly meaning 'land of salt'.

After its discovery by the Spanish neither they nor anyone else was much interested in the island for over a hundred years. It was visited from time to time by people of various nationalities in the early years of the seventeenth century but no one stayed until 1629. In that year a few French colonists arrived from St Kitts, which at that time was shared with the British. These settled in the northern part of the island near the east coast. They were followed within a year or so by some Dutch settlers who were interested in producing salt from the large pond behind Great Bay on the south coast. The two lots of settlers did not interfere with each other's activities and traded amicably until they were all ejected by the Spanish in 1633. The presence of other Europeans in what they considered to be their sole preserve was resented by the Spanish and, although they had no intention of developing the island themselves, it was barred to all other nationalities for the next 15 years. In 1648 as soon as the Spanish abandoned it for ever both the French and Dutch settlers returned, more or less simultaneously. This time relations between them were not so harmonious to begin with, and a brief skirmish took place before the two sides agreed to divide the island between them.

The division of the island

The agreement to do this was reached on 23 March 1648. It is not clear just how the two parties decided to draw the boundary between them, but what is certain is that it did *not* involve one man from each side walking around the island in opposite directions from the same starting point. This charming tale, suitably embellished with a description of the portly Dutchman stopping to drink his gin, and so covering less ground than the

The boundary monument on the French side . . .

. . . and on the Dutch side

wily Frenchman, is a myth which seems to have grown up at the same rate as the island's tourist industry. In fact the border was not established properly until well over a hundred years after the *Treaty of Morne des Accords*, as the 1648 agreement was called. Even then it was many years before a true demarcation took place.

The treaty was not always observed. The European wars of the seventeenth and eighteenth centuries, in which France and the Netherlands were involved, had their effect on St Martin and on the relationships between the people on either side of the non-existent border. When their mother countries were not at war the French and Dutch islanders had little to do with one another. Road communications across the border were very poor, and remained so until well into the present century. The general state of confusion concerning ownership came to an end in 1816, when the southern part of the island was handed back to the Dutch by the British after the last of their periodic occupations. The northern part had been returned to France in the previous year. From then on the political division was firmly established, and the friendly relationship between the two sides which then began has continued up until today. Even during the Second World War, when for a time Saint-Martin — as a dependency of Guadeloupe — gave nominal support to the Vichy regime in France, while Sint Maarten — together with the other colonies of the Netherlands — supported the Allies, there was no animosity. The peaceful 'occupation' of Sint Maarten in 1940 by 20 French soldiers, arrayed in puttees, knee-length khaki shorts and sola topis, who arrived in the back of a truck from Saint-Martin, was of extremely short duration. It came to an end in just over six weeks — probably because no one on either side could keep a straight face any longer. For the remainder of the war the islanders all suffered the same shortages of food and materials, but there was no real hardship. Perhaps the most important result of the war for the island was that in 1943 the United States paid for and constructed an airstrip on the flat land in the west of Sint Maarten. From then on St Martin had ready access to the outside world, and its occupants no longer depended solely on small boats or the infrequent ship for travelling abroad.

The original French settlement was at **Orléans** on the eastern side of the island, about 9 km from where the first Dutch settlers established themselves on **Simpson Bay**. Neither of these places was particularly suitable. Orléans was too far from the sea and Simpson Bay too far from the Great Salt Pond. This large pond is separated from the sea in Great Bay by a narrow sand bar, and it was here that the present capital was founded in 1733. It was not a perfect site, but at least the seaward approaches could be protected by a fort on either side of the entrance to Great Bay. The town was named after the Governor (or Commander as he was then called) who did much to develop the economy of Sint Maarten during his term of office from 1735 to 1746. That **Philipsburg** was named in honour of a Scotsman, John Philips, well illustrates the diverse origins of the early inhabitants. His tomb can still be seen among the ruins of an old church at **Cul de Sac**, in the centre of Sint Maarten. Later on in the eighteenth century the capital of Saint-Martin was established at **Marigot** on the west coast. This overlooked a large bay in which ships at anchor could be given some protection by a fort built behind the town on a hill. The name of the town is derived from the local word for a swampy puddle.

Marigot Harbour and waterfront

41

The long decline

As more settlers came to both sides of the island it was gradually divided up into plantations, initially for growing tobacco but soon for growing sugar-cane or raising livestock. By the middle of the eighteenth century all the original forest had been destroyed and the land laid out in fields. These often extended to the tops of the hills. Under the system of grants made by the early administrators land was divided into strips, and these were demarcated by walls

Wooden church in Philipsburg

made of the stones which the planters' slaves cleared from the fields between them. Many of these 'slave walls' can still be seen, particularly on the eastern slopes of the central range of hills in the Orléans area. They probably form the most enduring monument to the lives of the ancestors of many of the present-day inhabitants, just as the abandoned windmill towers do in some of the other Caribbean islands. By the end of the nineteenth century there were about 90 plantations. About half, mostly in Saint-Martin, were used for growing sugar-cane, while the rest were used for raising cattle and other animals.

The plantations were never very successful or profitable — the poor soil and low rainfall saw to that — and after the slave trade was made illegal in the early 1800s the chances of their becoming viable were reduced even more. By 1830 many had begun to fall into decay, and by the time the French abolished slavery in 1848 the end was in sight. Although the Dutch did not free their slaves for another 15 years it was difficult to prevent them escaping to freedom in Saint-Martin. After 1863 the island as a whole suffered from the breaking up of the plantation system. By the end of the century there were no more than a few hectares of sugar-cane being grown. Cotton was introduced and grown reasonably successfully for a while, but ceased to be profitable after about 1920. From then on agriculture played nothing but a minor part in the economy of the whole island.

The production of salt, the original 'crop' of the island, continued throughout the plantation era but with great fluctuations in demand and output. Most of it was harvested from the Great Salt Pond behind Philipsburg, and exported to North America and to other Caribbean islands. The heyday of the industry was reached in the middle of the last century, when at one time the Great Salt Pond produced up to four million kilograms of salt a year and created employment for about 1000 people. After that the industry slowly declined and ended altogether in 1949. The much smaller operation in Saint-Martin, based on the salt pond at Grand Case on the north-west coast, managed to keep going until 1967. The Great Salt Pond is now something of an embarrassment to Sint Maarten, being a large expanse of very shallow water, which soon becomes stagnant without frequent pumping and flushing procedures. Part of it

The Great Salt Pond behind Philipsburg, showing division of the salt-pans

immediately behind Philipsburg was filled in a few years ago to provide more land on which to build and room for a bypass road, but at some cost to the environment. Similarly, the pond at Grand Case was partially reclaimed in order to build the Espérance airstrip, but again with not much regard for aesthetic considerations.

The breakup of the plantation system and the abolition of slavery caused many people to leave, either to find work or to start a new life completely. Most of the white proprietors had left by 1880, going to Guadeloupe, Curaçao, Trinidad or the USA. The population declined steadily until the early years of the twentieth century, when about the same number of people — around 3500 — were left on either side of the border. This figure then remained more or less static for Saint-Martin, but decreased even more dramatically for Sint Maarten. This was brought about by the demand for workers at the newly-built oil refineries in Curaçao and, later, Aruba. Emigration remained a major fact of life for the islanders until well after the Second World War. By 1951 there were less than 1500 people left in Sint Maarten, with perhaps twice that number in Saint-Martin, with many on both sides of the border depending on remittances from overseas for their survival. To all outward appearances, and undoubtedly in the minds of many who lived there, St Martin was a forgotten and unwanted island.

Renaissance

The single most important factor which has transformed the island during the past 30 years has been the growth of the tourist industry. The lovely beaches, the considerable areas of unused and seemingly useless land, a terrain suitable for the construction of an international airport, the island's duty-free status, and the large number of nationals living overseas but only too willing to return home to work, all have contributed to the remarkable change which has taken place since 1955. This was the year in which the first tourist hotel, the **Little Bay Beach Hotel**, was built. It was not until many years later that the island started to realize its true potential. There was no constant public electricity supply until well into the 1960s, no proper air terminal until 1965, and no port facilities before 1964; the first bank in Philipsburg opened in 1960 but there was none in Marigot for another five years after that.

The development of tourism was assisted by events in the islands of Curaçao and Aruba, where automation of the oil refineries made many workers redundant. This provided the incentive for many of those from St Martin to return home. Some returned with sufficient means to build small guest-houses and apartments, to open stores and restaurants, and to provide the sort of goods and services required by North American tourists. Tourism came first to Sint Maarten and this is reflected today when the majority of resorts, hotels, restaurants and stores are found on the Dutch side of the border. Although today tourism means just as much to

Saint-Martin, because of its larger area the impact here has not been so marked.

The benefit to Sint Maarten from its lead in establishing a huge and thriving tourist industry has not been achieved without some cost to the environment. While on the French side it is easy to differentiate between the various hotels situated on individual beaches, this is becoming increasingly difficult on the Dutch side of the border. Virtually all of the south coast which is accessible has been, or is being, developed. Behind every beach between the westernmost point and Great Bay there are resorts, hotels, condominiums, villas and cottages jostling for space. Philipsburg has spread along the sand bar as far as it can in both directions and is now edging into the Great Salt Pond. Point Blanche peninsula, to the east of Great Bay, where it is not occupied by industrial concerns, yachting and port facilities, is gradually being covered with more tourist accommodation as well as private houses.

The accommodation already available includes some very sizeable resorts. The biggest, **Mullet Bay Beach Resort** at the western end of Sint Maarten, has hundreds of rooms and offers every facility from an 18-hole golf course and tennis-court complex

Oyster Pond Yacht Club

downwards. At the other end of the scale there are numerous self-catering cottages and apartments. The modern trend is towards the construction of condominium resorts in Sint Maarten, something which undoubtedly will spread to Saint-Martin as well. These are marketed as providing the owners with a complete vacation within the resort chosen, each development possessing its own restaurants, stores and sports facilities. Even though some of these resorts are very large, there has still been scope for even more grandiose development schemes in the past. The largest of all, which encompassed several multi-storey apartment blocks, an 800-room hotel, villas, restaurants, casino and yacht marina all interconnected by canals and cable-cars, was proposed for Little Bay in the late 1970s. Mercifully it seems to have suffocated under the magnitude of its conception. Such gigantic projects have not been restricted to the Dutch side, as can be seen in the folly of La Belle Creole just across the border on Marigot Bay. This is the unused and unfinished core of another huge development project, which envisaged a 300-room hotel in the midst of numerous villas and apartments. One is tempted to believe that if both of these projects had been completed St Martin by now would be tilting slowly into the Caribbean Sea ...

The island today

The relatively rapid growth of the tourist industry has had its effect on the whole of St Martin. With the understandable objective in mind of providing large numbers of tourists with a complete vacation 'package' the past has been ignored or forgotten. Other than the partially rebuilt walls of **Fort Amsterdam**, which used to guard Philipsburg, the overgrown ruins of **Fort Louis** overlooking Marigot, or the very slight and almost inaccessible remains of one or two other fortifications around Great Bay, there are no historical sites of any consequence. Neither Sint Maarten nor Saint-Martin has a museum. What old buildings remain, either in the towns or in the countryside, have to be sought out to be appreciated. The only 'sights', other than the ruined forts, the boundary monument, and a few attractive (if not so old) buildings in Marigot and Philipsburg, are natural ones.

Decorative canopy and shutters, Philipsburg

The standard tour of St Martin by bus or taxi, which is what most of the visitors accept and enjoy, takes no longer than two to three hours. This provides a reasonable view of the whole island and the chance to appreciate some of the splendid coastal scenery. For anyone who really wants to get to know the island this is far from adequate. To explore it properly will involve motoring in short stages, frequent stops, some walking and climbing, and a

The market, Marigot

determined effort to get to know — or at least to talk to — people not directly connected with the tourist industry. The total population is probably between 25 000 and 30 000 (it would seem that the precise figure is unknown even to the French and Dutch authorities, judging from the vastly differing numbers given in books and documents from both sides of the border), which is six times greater than it was 30 years ago. This enormous increase has done much to change the aspect of the island, particularly of the Dutch side. Buildings have proliferated everywhere and houses can be seen even on the steepest hillsides around the Great Salt Pond, as well as almost on top of Pic du Paradis. Much of the landscape has been changed out of all recognition, again especially around Philipsburg. Construction work everywhere has assisted in eradicating a lot of the past.

However, there are still some areas which remain much as they were fifty or a hundred years ago, but they are not to be found beside the road which forms the tourist circuit of the island. To find this older and possibly more real St Martin the interested visitor will be by himself; there are very few signposts, literal or metaphorical. To reach the summit of **Pic du Paradis**, to visit **Marcel Bay** in the north-west or **Geneve Bay** in the south-east, or to find the 'old Spanish fort' and **St Peter's Battery** on **Point Blanche**, will all involve more information than can be obtained from the tourist bureaux. To see these places, and many others, will necessitate talking to and taking advice from local people.

The tourist literature which is available is plentiful and of a high standard, but it is designed to keep its readers on a fairly standard circuit of the island, involving not much more than hotels, beaches, restaurants and duty-free shopping. Many of the brochures boast of St Martin's 36 beaches, and they are right to do so. The long stretches of clean white sand found on every coast are its greatest natural asset. It says much for Sint Maarten that the beach in Great Bay — situated between the largest town on the island and water which is used by hundreds of yachts, dozens of large motor-launches from cruise ships, and a variety of commercial shipping — remains one of the most frequented. Great Bay is an interesting and busy place; for the visitor who likes to have something to occupy her attention while relaxing under a coconut tree with a rum punch the Philipsburg beach is hard to beat.

49

Yachts play an important part in the day to day life of the island, especially in **Great Bay** and **Simpson Bay Lagoon**. In other Caribbean islands like Antigua or St Lucia most yachting activity takes place away from the main town. This is not so in St Martin, where yachts and sailing form a pleasing backdrop to life in both Philipsburg and Marigot. The general informality of the international yachting community adds to the cosmopolitan atmosphere of both towns. Because of its small size, the boating facilities available, and the pleasant sea conditions which prevail for most of the time, St Martin also offers the ordinary tourist some interesting sailing experiences. Several charter boats offer day-trips around the island, to **Tintamarre** or **Pinel Islet** off the east coast, or to neighbouring islands. Besides giving the pleasure of sailing under what are usually ideal conditions, they are also the only means by which the visitor will ever be able to see much of the rugged coastline of Saint-Martin.

Shopping and eating

The cosmopolitan air of Philipsburg is given an additional flavour when passengers come ashore from the many cruise ships which visit the island. The majority land at the small pier in the middle of the waterfront from where they enter the main square and the well-known **Front Street**. This narrow street, running parallel to the beach, has stores, hotels, restaurants and offices along nearly its entire length. The stores offer an amazing variety of goods — everything from cheap clothing, liquor and electronic equipment to the most expensive jewellery, crystal and fashion-wear — all at duty-free prices. The types of restaurants cover an equally wide range, with menus from India, China, Italy, Indonesia, France and the Caribbean, as well as from Central Europe and North America. Front Street's bustling sidewalks, non-stop traffic, busy stores and exotic eating places, together with the lovely view of Great Bay seen from the veranda of one of the restaurants, is probably all that many cruise ship passengers ever see of St Martin. It will not be much, but it will be enough to give even the most hard-boiled sceptic amongst them a day to remember. Those who combine the pleasures of Front Street with a circular tour will not find much

Front Street, Philipsburg

more of the genuine island, but they may well be inspired to consider a future, longer visit, during which it will be possible for them to get to know St Martin and its inhabitants.

The impressive range of shops and fine restaurants in Marigot will of course be visited by many of the day visitors, but their main clientele comes from those enjoying a vacation on the island. The restaurants in Marigot and Grand Case, just 5 km away, offer French, Creole, Vietnamese and Spanish cooking. The top one or two are probably the best of all the eating places on the island. Which restaurants they are does not fall within the scope of this book to decide, but the gourmet will have little difficulty in finding them. All restaurants advertise widely and 'word of mouth' recommendations are as easy to come by in Saint-Martin as in any other part of France.

Sign outside Spritzer and Fuhrmann, Front Street

This sign outside a fast-food restaurant offers a message to diners

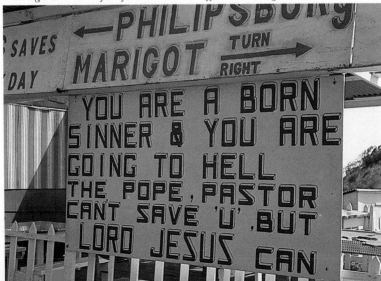

Felix Restaurant, Simpson Bay

The 'tourist industry façade'

The tourist industry of St Martin has made enormous advances in a relatively short period of time, often it would seem at the expense of other considerations. This is particularly so in Sint Maarten, which is smaller than its French counterpart but caters for far more tourists. The average visitor is likely to form the impression that there is nothing else on the island but tourism and that every aspect of life is geared towards its requirements. The huge resorts, the many hotels, the numerous beach cottages and apartments, the large range of attractions from casinos to water-sports, the ever-increasing number of stores and exotically-named eating places, all seem to have been allowed to multiply with scant regard for zoning or conservation. The tourist industry pays little attention to social and cultural considerations, and has expanded at the expense of any industrial or agricultural activity. While this has not yet created any serious problems, other than a more or less

The Mullet Bay Resort boasts an 18-hole championship golf-course

constant traffic jam in Front Street, it has erected an almost tangible barrier between the visitor and the ordinary life of the island.

The present trend towards condominium and time-sharing resorts can serve only to reinforce this barrier. It will become all too easy for the owner of a unit in one of these resorts to see the island as consisting of nothing more than the airport, Front Street and his own accommodation. St Martin has been turned into a superb vacation island in a little over one generation. The transformation has been carried out through the endeavours and goodwill of the present inhabitants, and much of the charm of the island lies in their mixed and colourful antecedents. To discover and enjoy all that it has to offer, the visitor will need to make a conscious effort to penetrate what I have termed the 'tourist industry façade'. To mix with and to get to know the people will at least provide an insight into how and why St Martin came to be what it is today. Just as there is more of the genuine life of

The Seaview Casino is one of many found in St Martin

Philipsburg to be seen in Back Street than among all the activity of Front Street, so there is much more to the 'Friendly Island' than the tourist brochures might lead one to believe.

For many visitors though, penetration of the 'façade' or even its dissolution will still not be enough. For those looking to the Caribbean for something more than sun, sea and sand — for something more taxing or adventurous, or even for a more intellectual type of vacation — St Martin will not be able to provide all that is sought. What it can provide though is an excellent base from which to search for the extra or missing dimension. It is a perfect jumping-off place for all the surrounding islands, and it is among these that the more discerning visitor will find the additional factor necessary for the ideal vacation. The two nearer islands are Anguilla to the north-west and Saint-Barthélemy to the south-east. The latter, although further away, is closer to St Martin in development and outlook; it is also the one which at present is more popular with day visitors.

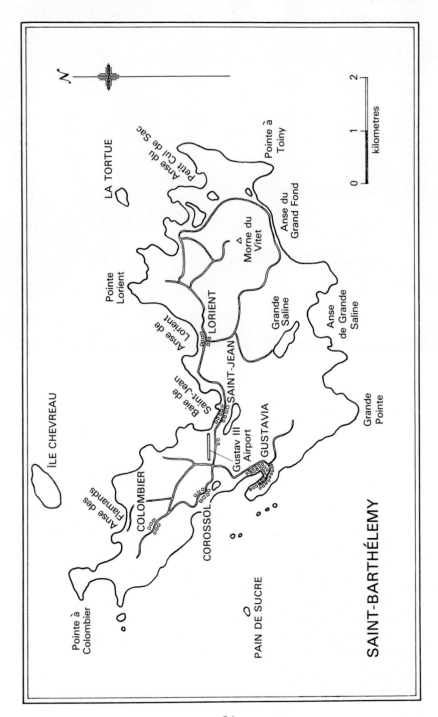

SAINT-BARTHÉLEMY

Chapter 6

The little pebble —
Saint-Barthélemy

The island

The small, boomerang-shaped island of Saint-Barthélemy is about 21 km from St Martin. In many ways it is a smaller version of its neighbour, with lots of hills, lovely beaches and an economy entirely dependent on tourism. But, because it is a wholly French island, there is an extra something about the way of life and its overall appearance which is not apparent even in Saint-Martin.

It is composed mainly of limestone with large areas of exposed rock. The hills are steep and covered with low trees and scrub, where they are not built upon. The valleys are mostly unused except for some grazing here and there among the scattered houses.

Saint-Barthélemy from the east

The highest point is about 280 m above sea-level towards the eastern end at **Morne du Vitet**. The whole island is no more than 25 square kilometres in area. It has no streams or lakes, and because of the limited rainfall an adequate supply of fresh water has always been a problem. There are salt ponds behind the beaches in several of the bays. The largest pond, **Grande Saline**, in the centre of the island was used to produce salt until modern times.

Saint-Barthélemy is surrounded by small islets and groups of rocks. The largest islet, **Fourchue**, is about 5 km to the north-west. It is deserted but visited regularly by yachtsmen.

Settlement of the island

A few pre-Columbian artefacts have been discovered on the island, but in view of the lack of permanent fresh water it is unlikely that the Amerindians had a permanent settlement. *Ouanalao*, as it was known to the Caribs, was deserted when the first Europeans landed. It was not discovered by Columbus, but may well have been named after Bartholomew, the great explorer's brother. It has been known by its present name since the beginning of the sixteenth century. The Spanish made no attempt to settle the island after its discovery and it was ignored until the middle of the seventeenth century. The first settlers, from the French part of St Kitts, arrived in 1648 in order to plant tobacco. The presence of Europeans in all the islands of the eastern Caribbean was resented by the Caribs, and the early settlers were frequently harassed. Those in Saint-Barthélemy were not spared and most of them were massacred in a raid of 1656. For a while the island was deserted but then resettled. By the end of the seventeenth century it had a population of around 500. By then the growing of tobacco had proved a failure. Other than being used for some cotton-planting and the raising of sheep and goats, the island's main use was as a base for buccaneers. During the European wars of the next century it changed hands on several occasions, always to the detriment of the inhabitants' attempts to create an ordered society and proper economy. Towards the end of the century it changed hands once again, this time not from the French to the British as a result of war, but peacefully to Sweden, in exchange for trading rights for France at Göteborg in the entrance to the Baltic.

Transfer to Sweden

Sweden took possession on 7 March 1785. The population then consisted of less than 500 whites together with about 280 slaves. The island was so poor that its principal asset was thought to be its goats, and these probably numbered less than the people. The Swedish authorities immediately made the island into a free port to take advantage of the increased trade flowing through the Caribbean as a result of the recently concluded American War of Independence. A proper port was created in the fine small natural harbour on the west coast and given the name **Gustavia** after King Gustav III of Sweden. From then on trade became the main economic activity. The island still got caught up in the Napoleonic wars from time to time, but prosperity increased as did the population. Within less than a quarter of a century after the Swedish take-over the population was well over 5000.

Despite the concentration on trade there was still some agricultural activity. Sugar-cane was planted but without much success, and farming took place in fairly small fields. The plantation system was never introduced and for most of the people outside Gustavia it is likely that life for both blacks and whites was not that different. Any agricultural activity under the adverse conditions created by a difficult terrain and lack of rain must have meant nearly as much work for the master as for the slaves. Again, it is probable that many of the farmers were in no financial position to afford more than one or two slaves. It is not surprising that, except briefly during the period of the island's greatest economic activity in the early nineteenth century, the black proportion of the population never exceeded that of the whites. By the time slavery was abolished by Sweden in 1847 there were only 520 slaves to be freed, and many of these soon left. They went because there was no work for them as free labourers and no land on which they could settle.

With the end of the Napoleonic wars in 1815 the economy of Saint-Barthélemy entered a long decline. Trade decreased and this caused many of the merchants to leave. A series of natural disasters, droughts, earthquakes and hurricanes, during the first half of the nineteenth century speeded the ruination of the economy. A huge fire devastated Gustavia in 1852, adding to the general distress. By 1870 the island was moribund, with no proper public services for a population of about 2400, and considered by Sweden to be nothing but a useless financial burden. In an attempt to get rid of the burden the Swedish Government approached the USA, Italy and France in turn. Only France showed any interest. The people of Saint-Barthélemy were given the opportunity to vote on whether to accept a return to French rule or not. Out of the 352 who were eligible, or who bothered to vote (and from the available evidence it is not clear which), only one dissented.

Return to France

Saint-Barthélemy was returned to French sovereignty on 16 March 1878. It made very little difference to the way of life and standard of living. The island continued to be a remote, forgotten and poverty-stricken place. That this poverty was not merely financial is surely borne out by the fact that it was not until the beginning of this century that the islanders started to import donkeys, to carry their goods along the trails which were then all that connected Gustavia with outlying communities. That it took until the twentieth century for the islanders to realize that these animals — which must have been in use in islands near by for the previous two hundred years or more — could be used to relieve man's burden, indicates either matchless obduracy or an incredible degree of torpidity among the population of the day.

The island remained in limbo until after the Second World War. During the war a state of general confusion seems to have existed. As a dependency of Guadeloupe, which was aligned with the Vichy Government until 1943, it suffered serious shortages of food, clothing and materials for four years. In the later stages of the war the islanders received intermittent supplies from St Kitts, St Thomas and Puerto Rico. Many people depended on assistance from relatives abroad, especially those in the US Virgin Islands. This period brought home to the inhabitants just how badly off they were in every respect. Once peace returned the island was ready for change and a chance to develop. With the redefinition of the status of the French West Indies in 1946 things began to improve slowly.

The advent of tourism

The first aircraft landed on Saint-Barthélemy in 1945, on an open grass field where the present airport is situated. This was the only possible landing place, then, as now. The pilot, Remy de Haenen, deserves a special place in the history of the region, not only for his contribution to the development of his native island, but also as a pioneer in inter-island communications. In the early days of the Second World War he started the first reasonably regular sea service between the islands, using two open motor-boats which he had built in Saint-Barthélemy, and which were known locally as the 'blue boats'. As soon as the war ended he saw the potential of the small airstrips which had been built by the US military authorities in Sint Maarten and St Kitts, and exchanged his boats for light aircraft. From a primitive base on Tintamarre Island off Saint-Martin he operated, for a time, an informal air service between the islands. He was instrumental in opening up both

Anse du Grand Fond

Saint-Barthélemy and Sint Eustatius to air travel, but probably his most memorable feat was to land the first aircraft on Saba, in 1959. In between his aviation exploits he also found time to open the first beach hotel in Saint-Barthélemy and to become the island's mayor for 15 years. Without his initiative and spirit of adventure it is likely that the modern history of the islands, Saint-Barthélemy and Saba in particular, might well have followed a different course.

The construction of an airstrip enabled the people of Saint-Barthélemy to take advantage of their proximity to St Martin, and even more of the common nationality they shared with the inhabitants of Saint-Martin. As tourists started to visit the larger island in increasing numbers in the 1960s many were inspired to spend a day in Saint-Barthélemy, just as they do now. The unspoiled attractions of the 'little pebble' (to use the affectionate

The Old Swedish Belfry

term coined by the island's historian Georges Bourdin) were broadcast, and a demand for tourist accommodation soon arose. The first hotel had been opened in 1953 — somewhat prematurely as it closed again within four years — but it was not until the early 1960s that the construction of tourist hotels as such was started. As the decade progressed the demand for accommodation soon outstripped the supply. At much the same time many wealthy North Americans seeking a secluded refuge from the North American winter saw the advantages of living in the Caribbean under the French flag, and began to buy land and houses. Proper public utilities, electricity, water and telephones, were provided in the same era. The tourist industry continued to expand and today it forms the basis of the economy. There are now over 30 hotels and guest-houses, together with all the usual facilities expected of a prestigious vacation resort.

It has been said that Saint-Barthélemy now has the highest per capita income of any island in the Caribbean. If this is true, and even a cursory tour of the island will provide many indications that it may well be so, then the transformation which has taken place in the last 30 years is even more remarkable than the change during the same period in its bigger neighbour to the west.

The island today

The population today is about 3000, the great majority being white. French of course is the official language, but English is spoken by anyone connected with tourism. The whole island has felt the impact of the tourist industry, but perhaps nowhere more than **Gustavia**. While this is still the capital the centre of life on the island has moved over the ridge behind the town to what used to be the tiny community of **Saint-Jean** on the north coast. This is the tourist centre, close to the airport, with numerous hotels, stores and restaurants, and on one of the best beaches. The road to Saint-Jean from Gustavia passes very close to the downwind end of the single airport runway. The airport, in defiance of good republican sentiments and modern convention, is named not just after a king but after a foreign monarch who died more than a century before the Wright brothers took to the air. **Gustav III**

Yachts anchored in Gustavia Harbour

Airport is named in honour of the Swedish king who granted the island its status as a free port in 1785. As this has been jealously guarded ever since, and has much to do with the island's present affluence, the name perhaps is not too incongruous.

The runway starts at the foot of a steep ridge and ends at the very edge of the **Baie de Saint-Jean**. This makes for an interesting arrival and an equally enthralling departure. One of the 'sights' is to watch aircraft landing from the top of the ridge, and this may be done very easily from beside the road. Air traffic is restricted to small aircraft carrying no more than 20 passengers. Landing takes place with the plane skimming the brow of the ridge (and all the sightseers) and then dropping abruptly on to the runway. Departure involves the plane making use of every metre of the runway before leaving the ground at the edge of the sea, and then banking sharply to the north to avoid the hills on the opposite side of the bay. All aircraft movements are equally exciting for both those in the air and those watching from the ground. Despite this — or even possibly because of it — the airport handles well over 16 000 movements a year and more than 100 000 (albeit perhaps slightly apprehensive) passengers.

Once on the ground, even if his heart is still somewhere in the air, the visitor immediately is aware that he is on a different kind of Caribbean island. The absence of black faces, the armed gendarme who inspects the passports, the chatter and clink of ice cubes from the bar alongside the arrival gate, the whiff of a Gauloise, and of course the proverbial soupçon of *je ne sais quoi* that is found in any part of France — all combine to greet him. This first impression is reinforced as soon as one leaves the airport terminal. Even the road traffic is different. There are none of the huge American motor cars which are only too prevalent in other small islands of the region. The automobiles which are seen are driven, for the most part, with a panache which is certainly not evident in neighbouring islands. Saint-Barthélemy is a tiny place, with roads that are narrow and in many places steep and twisting. Regardless of this there are few traffic accidents, and the island is free of that blight of nearly every other Caribbean island, the abandoned car at the roadside.

The hotels, the restaurants, the stores, the public buildings, the private houses, all fit into the scheme of things. There are no multi-storey buildings, and outside Gustavia it is impossible to find anything more than one storey high. There are no large hotels or resorts. The biggest hotel has no more than 50 rooms, the majority

Rue de la République, Gustavia

Sunbathing on a shell beach

have less than 20. The restaurants, as one would expect in any part of France, are many and varied and offer a wide range of menus and prices.

The tourist literature insists that Saint-Barthélemy has 22 beaches. Of these only about half are easily accessible. They are on all sides of the island and each will have its special attraction for the visitor. Those that are less accessible will repay the effort involved in reaching them, which — given the size of the island — will not be that strenuous. The beaches and the endless lovely views to seaward which are obtained in driving or walking must be the main attractions.

There is very little of historical interest. **Fort Oscar** on the western side of Gustavia Harbour is not open to the public, and little remains of **Fort Gustav** on the opposite side of the harbour. The two historical monuments which receive the most publicity are the **Old Swedish Belfry** at the southern end of Gustavia, and the **'English Anchor'** at the head of the harbour. Neither is all that noteworthy. In the case of the Belfry, which is now a clocktower, the main point of interest seems to be that the door has been painted in two colours. *L'ancre anglaise* is a large Admiralty pattern anchor which may or may not be 200 years old. It was probably brought to Gustavia by accident on the towing line of a tug, and fished out of the harbour in 1981. That so much is made in Saint-Barthélemy of what elsewhere would be of no great interest surely gives an indication of the charm of the island, as

The 'English Anchor', Gustavia Harbour

well as of the refreshingly unsophisticated outlook of the inhabitants.

This pleasant simplicity is also found in an aspect of life on the island with which the guide books and tourist brochures make great play. This concerns the village of **Corossol**, a kilometre or so to the north of Gustavia. (That an identifiable, separate community can exist so close to the capital provides an excellent illustration of just how small Saint-Barthélemy is.) There, according to these sources, the more elderly women are to be seen dressed in Breton dress, wearing the traditional *Calèche* ('Kiss-me-not' bonnets), many engaged in making straw baskets and hats outside their homes, and waiting to have their photographs taken. This is pure hokum. There are indeed ladies in Corossol who from time to time put on traditional dress; there may be some who make articles out of straw; and no doubt there are one or two who would not object too much to being photographed. But for every visitor who obtains such a picture there will be a thousand who will walk or drive through the village without finding it any different from any other community on the island.

Saint-Barthélemy is a marvellous place and really does not need the adman's efforts to turn what must be an old and cherished part of the island's cultural heritage into a tourist attraction. The 'little pebble' is a fragment of France, with just the right amount of the

Typical old houses

West Indian outlook, tempered by the better aspects of the North American way of life. It is not only different from the surrounding islands but from the other French West Indian islands as well. No other island in the eastern Caribbean has as much to offer the tourist seeking the standard attractions of sun, sea and sand together with excellent accommodation, good eating and duty-free shopping, in such a confined space. For the visitor who needs a little more room in which to enjoy the natural attractions, and who can forgo the French cuisine and the cheap shopping, there is a much larger island less than 36 km away on the opposite side of St Martin.

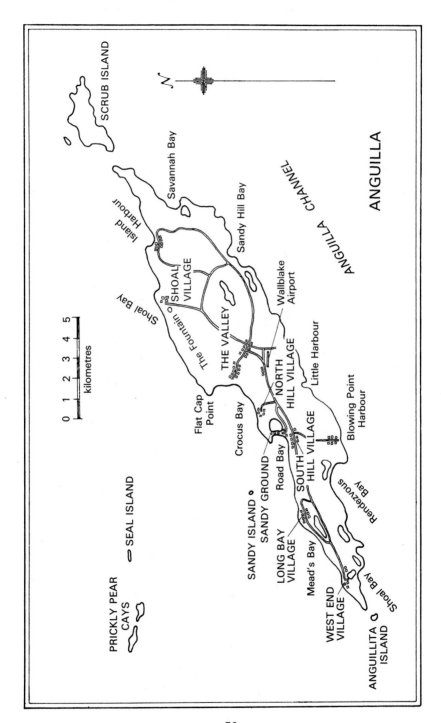

SCRUB ISLAND

Savannah Bay

Sandy Hill Bay

Island Harbour

Shoal Bay

SHOAL VILLAGE

The Fountain

THE VALLEY

Wallblake Airport

Flat Cap Point

Crocus Bay

NORTH HILL VILLAGE

Little Harbour

ANGUILLA CHANNEL

Blowing Point Harbour

SEAL ISLAND

SANDY ISLAND

SANDY GROUND

Road Bay

SOUTH HILL VILLAGE

Rendezvous Bay

PRICKLY PEAR CAYS

LONG BAY VILLAGE

Mead's Bay

WEST END VILLAGE

Shoal Bay

ANGUILLITA ISLAND

ANGUILLA

N

0 1 2 3 4 5
kilometres

Chapter 7

The undiscovered island — Anguilla

The island

Anguilla is about the same size as St Martin, but of a quite different shape and appearance, being long, narrow and very flat. It is another limestone island, with some very small outcrops of volcanic rock. In the distant geological past it was part of a low coastal plain extending westwards from the hills of St Martin. The Anguilla Channel which now separates the two islands is no more than 8 km wide and less than 20 m deep. Most of the island has just a thin layer of poor soil in which nothing but thorn scrub will grow without an excessive amount of attention. Here and there are small areas of much more fertile soil called 'bottoms'. The highest point is on the west coast at **Crocus Hill**, a flat-topped rise no more than 65 m above sea-level. Because it is so low Anguilla has the lowest rainfall of all five islands, probably an average of no more than about 900 mm a year. The somewhat depressing physical aspect is echoed in the name of the islet off the northern point — **Scrub Island,** and also in the names of others to the west — **Prickly Pear Cays** and **Dog Island.** Yet another islet some 55 km to the north-west belongs to Anguilla. Although it has a much more cheerful-sounding name, **Sombrero,** it too is low, flat and barren. The two factors which alleviate this rather uninviting prospect are Anguilla's magnificent beaches, and the exceptional character of the Anguillan people. The beaches have evolved and matured in splendour over many millions of years; the Anguillans have evolved as a recognizable group during little more than three centuries, perhaps only reaching maturity during the last two decades.

The magnificent circular sweep of Rendezvous Bay

Settlement of the island

As in St Martin and Saint-Barthélemy it was the various Amerindian people who were the first inhabitants of the island, and its Carib name was *Malliouhana*. Pre-Columbian remains have been found in numerous places all around the coast and on some of the offshore islets, but no full-scale archaeological survey has been carried out as yet. Because of some unique discoveries at one particular site, which will be mentioned in more detail later, it now seems probable that Anguilla may have been visited by large numbers of Amerindians for ceremonial purposes. However, because of the lack of fresh water — even more acute here than in any of the other islands — it is difficult to believe that it could ever have supported a large permanent population.

It is another island which was not discovered by Columbus, being much too low-lying to have been sighted from the route taken during his voyage of 1493. From the time of its first sighting by a European, whenever that was, the island was called Anguilla, after its vague resemblance to an eel. Whether it was first explored by a Spaniard, a Frenchman, or even an Italian (the word for an eel is very similar in all three languages) no one will ever know. After its discovery it was virtually ignored until early in the seventeenth century. Even then it was only because a few Dutch-men had gone there, shortly after the first settlement was established in St Martin, and built a small fort. When the Spanish ejected the French and Dutch from St Martin in 1633 they also demolished this fort. From then on Anguilla was visited only briefly from time to time by the odd Spaniard or Dutchman until a party of English settlers arrived in 1650. Although a contemporary description called the island so barren as to be 'scarce worth the planting' the settlers attempted the inevitable tobacco crop, collected salt from the salt ponds, and gradually created a proper community. It is more than likely that these original settlers were more or less outcasts; people who could not make a living in other islands where conditions were better, or who had some difficulty fitting in to an ordered society.

By the time the island was recognized as being a British possession and incorporated with neighbouring islands such as Antigua and St Kitts into one colony in 1671, the few inhabitants lived, as an eighteenth century historian put it very succinctly, 'without Government or Religion, having no Minister nor Governor, no Magistrates, no Law, and no Property worth keeping.' The British Government took no great interest in the island and for a hundred years or more the inhabitants were subjected to raids by various marauders and several attacks by the French. It was captured by the French for a while in the 1680s, but a subsequent attempt in 1745 was beaten off. This episode, during which a very small force of militia repulsed a much superior French invading force, was indisputably the highlight of Anguillan history until very recent times.

In between coping with desperadoes and beating off invasions the white Anguillans attempted to make a living from the land. Slaves were imported but not in any large numbers. Some plantations were established but not with any success; the island was too dry for growing a decent sugar crop and the soil generally unfit for intensive farming. Even before the end of the eighteenth century many of them had been abandoned. With little work available for them, many of the slaves were allowed to leave Anguilla, and to work abroad for enough money to buy their freedom. When they returned and became free men they were sometimes in a position to buy land and property. By the time slavery was abolished in the British colonies in 1834 the population consisted of no more than 300 whites, 300 'free coloureds', and about 3000 blacks. The island then entered a period of 'great distress', the few plantations which still existed produced next to nothing, and the majority of the white proprietors soon left. The sugar crop disappeared by the 1870s. The Anguillans, by then nearly all black or of mixed descent, survived by fishing, building boats, harvesting salt, trading in their boats between the islands, raising livestock, or by going abroad to work.

Emigration and the economy

Even before slavery was abolished it was necessary for Anguillans to find work abroad in order to support themselves and their families. Long periods of exile or separation have been a major factor in the social life of the island throughout nearly all its recorded history. In the middle of the nineteenth century, when large phosphate deposits were discovered on Sombrero Island, Anguillan labourers were able to work a little nearer home. Normally — and the phosphate mining operation did not remain profitable for very long — they had to go much further afield. They provided sugar-cane cutters in places like Cuba and the Dominican Republic, as well as in St Kitts. Many went to the US Virgin Islands and to the USA. When the first oil refineries were planned in Curaçao and Aruba, Anguillans joined their neighbours in the Dutch islands in providing the labour needed to construct and operate them. In more recent times large numbers emigrated to Great Britain. Today there are at least as many Anguillans living overseas as there are on the island. For over 150 years the economy has depended to a great extent on remittances from abroad.

By the middle of the twentieth century Anguilla was a rather strange place, with a people, character and economy unlike that of any other British West Indian island. Because of the poor soil and low rainfall agricultural activity had practically ceased to exist. Something like 80 per cent of the population were unemployed except for growing a few subsistence crops and raising one or two animals. At the same time land ownership was very widespread. Few people were wealthy but even fewer lived in poverty. Those living abroad maintained close links with their relatives on the island, and many returned at the end of their working lives to live in houses built in slow stages over the years. At the same time Anguilla lacked even the most basic amenities and, to everyone but the inhabitants, appeared to be a wretched and economically useless island. In this respect it resembled its immediate Dutch and French neighbours far more than it did the British islands of St Kitts and Nevis, to which it had been affiliated since the earliest days of the settlement.

Affiliation with St Kitts

From 1671 Anguilla formed part of a colony which included not only St Kitts and Nevis, but also Montserrat, Antigua and Barbuda. After 1815 when the ownership of all the Caribbean islands had been sorted out finally, the British colonial set-up was reorganized. Anguilla was annexed to St Kitts and administered as part of a colony which initially included Nevis and the Virgin Islands. Later they were joined to Antigua, Barbuda, Montserrat and Dominica in a single Leeward Islands Colony. Still later this colony was split into a number of 'Presidencies', each with its own Administrator. In 1882 Anguilla was united with St Kitts and Nevis in a single Presidency. This association of Anguilla with St Kitts, was, from the beginning, made for the convenience of the colonial authorities, and with no regard for the wishes of the Anguillans themselves. From time to time the islanders appealed

75

to the British Government to separate the island from St Kitts, but always without success.

The one real opportunity for separation and developing what agricultural potential the island possesses came about in 1891. In that year the Governor of the Leeward Islands proposed that Anguilla be joined to Barbuda (a much bigger island about 150 km to the south-east) as a separate colony. He argued in his submission to the British Colonial Office that both islands could then be developed as producers of livestock, and that this could then be exported to other islands. Needless to say, as this would have involved the Colonial Office in providing a capital sum for the purchase of breeding stock and transport, it was rejected out of hand. Had it not been, it is interesting to speculate not only on the difference this would have made to the subsequent history of Anguilla, but also on what might have become of Barbuda, the much smaller and grossly under-developed part of the unitary state of Antigua and Barbuda. Certainly the people of both islands had and have much more in common than the Anguillans do with the people of St Kitts, or the Barbudans with those of Antigua.

And so Anguilla, through the parsimony of the British Government, and in spite of the wishes of the people, remained tied to St Kitts, an island almost as far away as Barbuda. The two islands had little in common. The economy of St Kitts was founded entirely on sugar, with an estate system creating fixed social barriers between a few landed proprietors and a large, landless peasant labour force. Sugar and estates were unknown in Anguilla where, by the end of the nineteenth century, the majority of people owned land and property. In spite of this Anguillans were always treated very much as 'poor relations' and given only nominal representation in the House of Assembly in St Kitts. The Anguillan resentment increased as the years went by. The creation in 1956 of the separate colony of St Kitts, Nevis and Anguilla, under its own Governor, did nothing to lessen the resentment. On the contrary the dissatisfaction increased as the colony moved towards political independence during the 1960s. During this period many Anguillans returned from working in Curaçao and Aruba, where the oil refineries were reducing their labour-force, and saw for themselves how far the island lagged behind others in the region in even basic public services. Resent-

76

ment came to a head in 1967 when the colony was granted independence 'in association with Great Britain', with full internal self-government.

The rebellion

As soon as 'Statehood' was proclaimed on 27 February of that year the people of Anguilla rebelled against the new government based in Basseterre, the capital of St Kitts. They asked for 'self-determination' with complete separation from St Kitts, and a return to direct British rule as an interim measure. This act, which involved the deportation of the Warden and most of the police force, was the beginning of a period of general confusion which lasted until 1982. During these 15 years Anguillans held two referendums and four general elections, carried out a ludicrously inept 'invasion' of St Kitts, were 'invaded' in turn by British troops, ejected a British envoy, and drew up various constitutions (at least one of which was of the most dubious provenance). The net results were achieved at widely spaced intervals. In 1971 the British Government passed an Act recognizing the reality of the separation of the island from St Kitts, and providing for its administration by a Commissioner. This was followed in 1976 by the Anguilla (Constitution) Order, which introduced a ministerial form of government. The formal separation of Anguilla from St Kitts was delayed until 1980 when a second Anguilla Act was passed by the British Parliament. Finally, in 1982, the island was granted its present constitution and the Commissioner was replaced by a Governor. Anguilla is now, as its tourist brochures proudly state, 'a British colony' and one of the very few places in the world still content with that designation.

The political events of the years since the rebellion of 1967 have had a profound effect on the Anguillans. They have also brought about major changes to the face of the island. It now has a proper road system, an island-wide electricity supply, a comprehensive internal telephone system, and reliable telecommunications with the rest of the world. The public water supply has been greatly extended and improved, with new storage tanks and the incorporation of a reverse osmosis plant. A new hospital is planned, and a technical and vocational training college is being built. The abrupt severance of any political connection with St Kitts can be regretted by very few, if any, of the population. Even the increasing number of British tourists, whose taxes have contributed to the present development, can hardly fail to agree that the break was all to the good.

The Valley

The largest community on the island — with several hundred houses, one or two churches, a few small shops, and various government offices — is situated in a shallow valley inland from Crocus Bay about half-way along the west coast. This is the administrative centre; the words 'capital' or even 'town' being quite inappropriate. It is called simply **The Valley**. It is not clear from the little information available about the early days of the settlement just where the first Europeans lived. It is probable that they established themselves either near **Sandy Hill Bay** on the east coast, or near the main salt pond at **Road Bay** on the opposite side of the island. How The Valley acquired its present status seems equally uncertain, but it is very symptomatic of the

The only set of traffic-lights on the island, at The Valley

disregard with which the island was treated in colonial days that no recognizable capital with a proper name was ever founded or even planned. On the other hand, the absence of a genuine town does have its advantages. To a greater extent than in all of the other ex-British West Indies, all Anguillans are villagers. There is none of the 'town versus country' feeling which is prevalent among the inhabitants of many another island where there is a capital town or city whose inhabitants see themselves, for no very good reason, as socially superior to the people of the outlying villages.

Ports

There are three ports of entry — the airport and the seaports at **Sandy Ground** and **Blowing Point. Wallblake Airport** is less than 2 km from The Valley. Like the airport in Sint Maarten the original airstrip was built during the Second World War by the US military authorities. Commercial flights did not begin until 1956, and now the airport handles around 10 000 aircraft movements a year. The present terminal building is due to be replaced in 1987. The majority of visitors who intend to stay for more than one day arrive by air, probably numbering about 20 000 each year.

Arrival at Wallblake Airport

Another forty or fifty thousand people visit for just one day, using the ferry service which operates between Marigot in Saint-Martin and **Blowing Point Harbour** on the south coast. This service has developed only since 1980. Before then there were a few auxiliary-powered sloops which made infrequent crossings, but these have been replaced by fast motor boats running to a fixed schedule. As a result Blowing Point has become the main passenger port of the island. **Sandy Ground** at Road Bay on the opposite coast is the main cargo port. There, the small jetty and rather rudimentary cargo-handling facilities are due to be enlarged and improved within the next couple of years.

The sea and boats

Since very early days the sea has played a major part in the life of the Anguillan people. Because many of them were forced to travel abroad to find work they became accustomed to the sea and ships. For many of those left behind, fishing, trading and boat-building provided a livelihood. The Anguillans are a seagoing people — far more so than the inhabitants of St Kitts or even the much closer St Martin. Their reputation as boat-builders is equalled in the eastern Caribbean only by the people of the Grenadines. Of the five islands which form the subject of this book, only Saba has produced men with a greater affinity for the sea. Small coasters owned and crewed by Anguillans can still be found trading

Fishermen hauling in their nets at Sandy Ground Village

throughout the region, and fishing on the Anguilla Bank is still a full-time occupation for many islanders.

This close relationship with the sea is borne out by the fact that the national sport is not (as in every other West Indian island which is or has been owned by the British) cricket, but boat racing. Races between undecked wooden sloops built to a traditional design (for which no drawings have ever existed) take place several times a year. The main ones are during the first week in August, which is also Anguilla Carnival Week. Others are run on Anguilla Day in May, at Easter and on New Year's Day. They take place at various points around the island and are very competitive. At the same time the actual venues, the number of entrants, the starting times, the lengths of the courses, and everything else to do with the races, are all decided with a flexibility and a degree of informality which accords well with the Anguillan character. Even if the racing is highly competitive each race day is entirely uncommercialized, and provides much fun and relaxation for participants and spectators alike.

Salt

In Anguilla the salt ponds are just as much in evidence as they are in St Martin and Saint-Barthélemy, but here the harvesting of a salt 'crop' is not yet a thing of the past. In Sandy Ground Village vast piles of salt can be seen alongside the road, and the small grinding and bagging plant towards the northern end of the village still operates occasionally. The production of salt, mainly for industrial purposes, is still a feature of the Anguillan way of life, although its export has declined greatly in recent years. The actual process of harvesting, using casual labour working from large wooden punts on Road Bay Pond, cannot have changed significantly since the earliest days of the settlement. The contrast between this archaic industry and the surrounding modern life of Anguilla, with its large houses, well-appointed hotels and expensive yachts, needs no stressing. But contrasts like this are very much part of the island's charm. Salt has played an extremely important part in its history, and if the industry is now abandoned an essential part of the character of Anguilla will be taken away.

Bagging salt from the Great Road Salt Pond

The island's attractions

The main emphasis of the Anguillan tourist industry is towards providing for visitors from, as the Government's tourism policy document puts it, 'the upper stratum of the world travel market'. Large resort developments geared towards the provision of 'package holidays' are not permitted, and neither are casinos. The present tourist accommodation — practically all of which has been built during the last decade — consists of nine hotels, a similar number of guest-houses, and perhaps 30 villa, cottage or apartment complexes. None of the hotels has more than 41 rooms. The accommodation is spread all around the island, mostly on or very close to a beach.

A typical Anguillan house

The beaches — extremely long stretches of pure white sand — are without doubt the island's main asset and tourist attraction. Of the total coastline of about 70 km, between one quarter and one third consists of beaches. Nearly all of them are accessible by road, while the remainder can be reached without too much effort on foot. If this is not enough there are another 26 kilometres or so of beach to be found on the off-lying islets and cays. All of these can be easily reached by one of the many boats which are for charter. **Sandy Island**, about 3 km west of Sandy Ground, is the most accessible and for that reason the most popular. **Seal Island, Prickly Pear Cays** and **Dog Island**, which are all further away to the west, offer even better beaches as well as some of the finest diving and snorkelling conditions in the region. Dog Island also has the remains of an old farmhouse and other signs of past habitation to be explored.

The most distant island, **Sombrero**, is also the one on which it is most difficult to land. Called the 'Spanish Hat Island' by the sailors of long ago it lies in the middle of the northern end of the Sombrero Channel. This is one of the main entrances into the Caribbean Sea for shipping from Europe. The island is just over one kilometre in length and less than half a kilometre wide, with eroded limestone cliffs on all sides. It is treeless, waterless and without any animal life other than large lizards and seabirds. In 1807 a British seaman named Robert Jeffery was marooned there for some misdemeanour committed in his ship HMS *Recruit*. He survived for over a week before being rescued by a passing American ship. After his return to England he was awarded compensation for his sufferings, while the captain of his ship was dismissed from the Royal Navy. Later on in the 1800s the large deposits of guano on the island were mined for some years, being shipped to the USA for use as fertilizer. The quarries and spoil heaps are still visible.

Because of its key position a lighthouse was built on the island in 1869. This remained in operation until the 1960s when it was replaced by the present tower and buildings. The lighthouse is manned by Anguillan keepers, and operated on behalf of the international shipping community by the Corporation of Trinity House, the maritime authority responsible for lights and buoys around the English coasts. A visit to Sombrero involves a boat journey of several hours across a stretch of water which is frequently capricious, to say the least. For anyone with good sea-legs, and who is interested in seeing one of the more remote and unusual of the Lesser Antilles, this should not be too much of a deterrent.

The only other natural attraction of any importance in Anguilla is **The Fountain**, near Shoal Bay on the north coast. This is the somewhat misleading name for a large dome-shaped cave which contains a constant supply of fresh water. In days gone by this was the only source of water in the area. To obtain access people had to climb up and down the roots of a big 'Gum Apple' tree which grows over the narrow entrance. These roots descend some 10 m into the cave before reaching the floor. There is now an iron ladder alongside the roots, which was put there to improve access for the water carriers. That this was erected in recent times, while the island was still part of the colony of St Kitts, Nevis and Anguilla, surely says more than any number of words about the backwardness of Anguilla before the 1967 rebellion, and the contempt with which the Anguillans were treated by the then Government of St Kitts. Today the fresh water is of little importance compared with the great archaeological significance of

84

The Fountain. Within the last ten years surveys have shown that the cave contains some outstandingly interesting Amerindian rock carvings, or petroglyphs, as well as numerous artefacts. The Fountain now 'promises to be a site of substantial regional importance' in the study of the pre-Columbian history of the Lesser Antilles. Because of this the cave and the surrounding area are being developed as a national park. By 1988 it is hoped that the cave will be re-opened to the public, with access through a museum which will be built above it.

The 'best-kept secret'

Of the three islands on the Anguilla Bank, Anguilla not only has the newest and smallest tourist industry, but also the greatest potential. With an area almost the same as that of St Martin, and a population only a quarter of the size, the scope for development is considerable. The present annual total of day visitors is barely half that of those who visit Saint-Barthélemy for a similar period, even though Anguilla is much closer to St Martin. The number of tourists who stay for more than a day is derisory when compared with the figures for Sint Maarten, Saint-Martin or Saint-Barthélemy. The Tourist Department's description of Anguilla as 'the Caribbean's best-kept secret' is still very valid. It has to be

Cinnamon Reef Beach Club

admitted that from a distance the island looks unprepossessing, especially when contrasted with the gentle hilly outline of its neighbour across the Anguilla Channel. Again, no one — least of all an Anguillan — would claim that The Valley held any attraction when compared to Philipsburg, Marigot or Gustavia. But Anguilla does have its appeal, and it has to be lived in for a while before it can be appreciated. Much of its interest and allure is to be found through the Anguillan people, and in sharing something of the secret they have kept to themselves for the past 300 years. For outsiders it is still very much the 'undiscovered island', in the sense that it has all the natural attractions of a classic tropical tourist resort, but is not yet visited by more than a handful of tourists.

About 75 km to the south is another island which also can be thought of as 'undiscovered', but this time in a rather different sense. Sint Eustatius has few of the features of a Caribbean tourist resort. It is an island with its own special appeal, part of which is a richer and far more interesting history than any of the other islands. It is in looking into this history, and in enjoying the aura of the past which is diffused by the whole island, that the discovery of Sint Eustatius is to be made.

Chapter 8

The golden rock —
Sint Eustatius

The island

Shaped like a slightly distorted pear lying on its side, Sint
Eustatius is about 13 km to the north-west of St Kitts, to which it
is joined by a bank of relatively shallow water. Although it is only
about 21 square kilometres in area it is divided into three distinctly
different topographical regions. The northern third consists of
sparsely covered hills with steep-sided valleys or 'guts', and is
completely uninhabited. The whole of the southern third of the
island is a regularly-shaped extinct volcano called **The Quill**, after
the Dutch word *kuil* for a pit or hollow. The Quill's classic,
concave slopes and wide, deep crater make it, as the authoritative
geological report on the island states, 'perhaps the finest example
of its kind in the Antilles'. Its highest point is just over 600 m
above sea-level. Between the northern hills and The Quill is a low,
flat plain which stretches from one side of the island to the other,
ending in cliffs on either coast. This is called the *Cultuurvlakte* or
agricultural plain — now something of a misnomer in view of the
tiny amount of farming which takes place here. Until recent times
this was the only inhabited portion of the island, where all
agricultural and commercial activity took place. Today houses are
to be seen scattered on the lower slopes of The Quill on the north
and west sides, and a large oil trans-shipment terminal has been
constructed among the hills at the western end of the island. Sint
Eustatius is alone among the five islands in having no offshore
islets, and the approaches to it are free from any underwater
dangers except very close inshore.

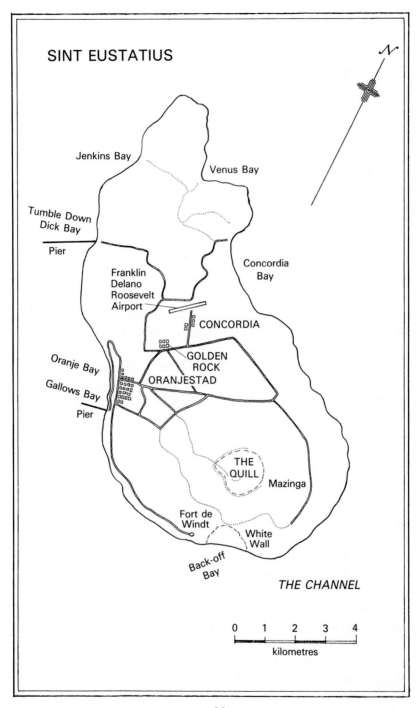

SINT EUSTATIUS

Jenkins Bay

Venus Bay

N

Tumble Down
Dick Bay

Pier

Concordia
Bay

Franklin
Delano
Roosevelt
Airport

CONCORDIA

Oranje Bay

GOLDEN
ROCK

ORANJESTAD

Gallows Bay

Pier

THE
QUILL

Mazinga

Fort de
Windt

White
Wall

Back-off
Bay

THE CHANNEL

0   1   2   3   4

kilometres

The Quill

Discovery and settlement

The Amerindians of course were the first inhabitants. Some evidence of their occupation of the island has been unearthed at one or two sites on the central plain, and dated to about AD 300. The Carib name, based on very slender evidence, was something like *Aloi*, but the island received its present name on 12 November 1493 from Christopher Columbus. He named it, as he sailed past to the south, after the virgin martyr St Anastasia. This was later corrupted into *Sant Estacio* and then became Sint Eustatius when the Dutch settled there in 1636. At that time it was uninhabited although the French had made a brief attempt to found a settlement seven years earlier. Inevitably, just as in the other islands, tobacco was the first crop to be planted, and just as inevitably it proved to be a failure. All attempts to grow anything on a commercial scale, whether it was tobacco, or later, sugar, coffee or cotton, were set back by the poor rainfall and by repeated attacks and invasions. These continued throughout the first 180 years of the island's recorded history; between 1636 and 1816 it changed hands between the Dutch, French and British no less than 22 times. The Dutch occupied it for longer than anyone else but it was the six British occupations, lasting for a total of about 22 years, which left the most lasting impression. Each change of ownership involved the usual destruction of property, plunder and deportations, but in the end the turmoil produced a very mixed population with English as their first language.

The golden era

From about the middle of the eighteenth century trade became the most important factor in the life of the island. Profiting from its position in the midst of islands owned by the British, French, Spanish, as well as the Dutch, and on busy shipping routes from Europe and North America, it soon became a key trading port. The number of plantations — the high-sounding term for what were probably never more than small and unproductive farms — decreased rapidly as trade and commerce took over. Trading in sugar, tobacco and cotton was found to be far more profitable than trying to grow them. The buying and selling of slaves was much more congenial than having to feed, house and clothe them while they struggled to make a plantation pay its way. Soon every type of commodity was being handled, and Oranjestad, which was the only town, became a thriving trans-shipment port. Sugar was the main export. Nearly all of it was shipped illegally — in contravention of the restrictions imposed by the governments of the countries that owned them — from the neighbouring islands. The ships from Europe and North America which came for sugar brought cargoes of every sort including slaves, salted fish, gunpowder, cloth, wine and household goods. All import duties were abolished in 1756 and Sint Eustatius entered its golden era as the busiest and richest island in the eastern Caribbean. Anything up to 2000 ships called each year. The houses and warehouses of the merchants — Dutch, English, French, Jewish, Spanish, Greek and Levantine — occupied all the beach front of the bay below Oranjestad, on both sides of the road through what was called Lower Town. The population, which in 1715 had been no more than 1200, had swelled to about 8000 by 1780. More than half of these were slaves.

That Sint Eustatius became such an important trading centre

seems remarkable considering the practical aspect of actually transferring goods to and from the hundreds of ships which anchored off Oranjestad each year. They had to anchor in a stretch of water which hardly deserves the title of a bay, and which is open to the sea and swell from the north, south and west. **Oranje Bay** has always been recognized as a poor and uncomfortable anchorage. The swell causes ships to roll and creates a surf along the shore which makes landing difficult, and at times dangerous. The prevailing sea conditions prevented any sort of landing jetty being built until early in the nineteenth century, and this was soon destroyed. All subsequent attempts came to nothing until the present pier was constructed as recently as 1976. Even this, despite its size and solid construction, has its use limited by rough seas; in 1985 it was damaged by heavy swells caused by a passing hurricane.

From the first settlement, and throughout the heyday of the island right up until modern times, everything brought to Sint Eustatius by sea had to be transferred to small boats before being landed over the beach below Oranjestad. Often such landings were impossible and the crews of ships at anchor, waiting to load or unload, must have endured a lot of frustration and discomfort. The fact that all cargoes had to be handled in this way probably accounts for the presence of the blue beads, often referred to as 'slave beads', which are discovered from time to time on the beach at Lower Town. These are small glass prisms which were made in Europe in the seventeenth and eighteenth centuries for trading purposes in Africa. While it is inconceivable that they would have been used in any way for direct trading in Sint Eustatius, it is very likely that some of the ships engaged in the triangular trade between Europe, West Africa and the West Indies would have carried beads as a normal part of their cargo. It is only necessary to visualize the captain of one such ship, wishing to dispose of some unwanted beads in order to make room for more sugar, rum or whatever, sending a cask or sack ashore. If the boat was then overturned in the surf — which must have been a common enough occurrence — it is easy to understand how even 200 years later a few beads come to light now and then amongst the sand.

Regardless of its uncomfortable anchorage, the difficulties of landing and the absence of proper port facilities, Sint Eustatius by the last quarter of the eighteenth century had become the 'Golden Rock' of the Caribbean. With the outbreak of the American War of Independence in 1775 trade flourished as never before. But it was all too good to last. Before the close of the century the island's prosperity had disappeared — brought about in the main by two events which are now firmly established as the key incidents in the history of Sint Eustatius.

The *Andrew Doria* and the Great Union flag

Soon after the start of the American War of Independence ships from the American colonies began to arrive off Oranjestad in order to buy arms and ammunition brought from Europe. In November 1776 an armed brigantine, the *Andrew Doria*, anchored off Lower Town. It was commanded by Captain Isaiah Robinson, who had recently been given a commission as a Captain of the Navy by the Second Continental Congress in Philadelphia. This meant that although the ship was not technically a warship — having been 'taken up from trade' — it was commanded by a naval officer and as such it had to be considered a ship of war. On its arrival in Sint Eustatius it was flying the new flag of the rebel colonists, the Great Union flag. This was dipped in the time-honoured way as a mark of greeting to the commander of the fort ashore, and the Dutch flag was dipped in turn although no one in the fort had ever seen the Great Union flag before. The ship and fort then exchanged gun salutes as was the normal custom. As the *Andrew Doria* was in every respect a merchant ship to all outward appearances those ashore surmised, quite correctly, that it was a foreign vessel on a trading voyage. The exchange of salutes took place before anyone from the ship went ashore and the true identity and status of the crew were made known.

This routine event has since been made to appear of great significance. Over the years it has been transmuted into a delibe-rate act on the part of the then Governor (or Commander as he was called) of the island to acknowledge formally the existence of the United States of America, thus making Sint Eustatius the first country ever to recognize the new nation. This 'fact' is enshrined in the words on a plaque in Fort Oranje, the plaque having been presented by President Roosevelt in 1939. The words make very appealing reading today, while standing in the courtyard of the beautifully restored fort overlooking the turquoise Caribbean, with the island's flag fluttering overhead in the trade wind, but regrettably they serve only to perpetuate a myth. The salute given from the fort all those years ago was in reality no more than a courtesy salute by a foreign government to the American flag being flown from a United States naval vessel. It probably was not even the first such salute, but it is the first one with proper authentication. It certainly did not represent formal recognition of the USA by the Dutch or any other government. All the same the salute caused immense dissatisfaction in the British islands and in Great Britain when it became known. It increased the anger felt by the British Government at the amount of aid being supplied to the rebels through Sint Eustatius, and this anger continued to simmer until the beginning of 1781.

Admiral Rodney's attack and the aftermath

On 3 February of that year a large British fleet under the command of Admiral Sir George Rodney appeared off the island. Two officers from the flagship went ashore under a flag of truce to demand its surrender, and without a shot being fired Sint Eustatius fell into British hands for the fourth time in its history. All the merchant ships at anchor in Oranje Bay were captured, as well as a convoy which had sailed for Europe the day before (and so was soon overhauled by the British warships). In addition about another 150 vessels were seized during the following few weeks, as they arrived to trade unaware of the new situation. Admiral Rodney proceeded to hold an enormous auction of not only all the merchandise he found ashore, but of all the ships and their cargoes as well. This raised an immense sum of money, and ruined the merchants and many shipowners alike. It did not meet with universal approval however, and later Rodney was sued by a number of the merchants who were British subjects and attacked in the British Parliament for allowing a lot of the auctioned goods to fall into enemy hands. Fortunately, the Admiral — who rightly has been called one of the finest sea commanders of all time — had made a habit of winning battles throughout his career. After his decisive victory in the Battle of the Saintes in April 1782, which prevented the British West Indies from falling under French domination, he was given a peerage and the matter of the auction in Sint Eustatius was forgotten.

Well before the Battle of the Saintes took place the British garrison left behind in the island had been attacked and captured by the French. Sint Eustatius then remained in French hands until 1784. After their departure some of the prosperity of former days was regained, but not for very long. Between 1784 and 1816, when it was restored to the Dutch for the last time, the island changed hands another five times, with the inevitable effect of ruining the economy. By 1816 it had declined so much that most of the Lower Town warehouses had collapsed, and the population was reduced to less than 3000. Cultivation of the central plain once again became the main activity, but even this petered out as the abolition of slavery approached. After the emancipation of the slaves in 1863 the island went into an even greater decline, the reduced population struggling to exist on subsistence farming, occasional trading with passing ships, and remittances from those who had gone elsewhere to work. Attempts to grow cotton and sisal in the early years of the present century came to nothing with the outbreak of the First World War and the loss of potential markets. A number of schemes to mine and export minerals, volcanic earth, gypsum and pumice, met with the same lack of success. By 1939 the entire population of about 1000 lived in Oranjestad, and consisted mainly of the very old and the very young with a large surplus of women. The circumstances under which they lived had become so reduced that attempts to get some of them to move to new housing projects, even though these were within two or three kilometres of Oranjestad, failed because of the lack of roads and basic services.

The island today

This dismal situation continued to exist until well after the Second World War, and to some extent the effects are still felt today. Sint Eustatius is the least prosperous of all five islands. The population is now about 1600, and so nearly twice as large as at its lowest point in 1948. The amount of agricultural, industrial and commercial activity is still tiny. A small airstrip was built in 1946 in the centre of the island about 2 km from Oranjestad. This, together with the exploits of the pioneering Remy de Haenen and others like him, improved communications with the outside world but did little to bring about an economic recovery — at least until very recently. The airport facilities, which are still limited to daylight operations, were improved in 1960 and again eleven years later. The airfield, which was named in honour of **President Franklin Roosevelt** of the United States in 1964, handles small aircraft operating between Sint Maarten, Saba, St Kitts and St Thomas. The total number of passengers arriving each year is no more than about 13 000.

To travel from Sint Maarten to Sint Eustatius takes no more than 20 minutes by air, but to undertake the journey is to travel

The Moonshay Bay Publick House

backwards in time by at least 20 years. Anyone visiting these islands with an interest in the past, even if it is just in getting some idea of how St Martin looked before the advent of tourism, should visit Sint Eustatius. The main attraction of the island must lie in its timeless atmosphere and seemingly changeless appearance. From the moment of arrival at the airport (which closes down between the morning and afternoon flights) the impression of time having stood still is constantly being renewed. The main road connecting the airport with Oranjestad is a narrow lane. Most of the vehicles using it are not the sleek automobiles and mini-buses which now and then threaten to bring the traffic between Juliana airport and Philipsburg to a standstill, but belong to an age when motor cars were more sedate and those with an automatic gearbox were known colloquially as 'mash-and-go'. Oranjestad has no traffic problem. The roads are in reality pleasant footpaths along which the odd vehicle passes now and then. For anyone used to ordinary town or city life in any other country, to be able to stroll anywhere in Sint Eustatius without constantly having to worry about 'the traffic' is a keen pleasure.

For the visitor who stays for more than one day the unusual history of the island must be one of the prime attractions. In recent years steps have been taken to preserve as much as possible of the old houses, fortifications and monuments which have played a part in that history. The full potential of the numerous historic sites has still to be realized however, and a lot of history is still being unearthed. (Quite literally in some cases. I was on the island in 1982 when the foundations were being dug for a new building among the ruins of Lower Town. Numerous artefacts from the 'Golden Rock' era were being uncovered and collected by the enthusiastic, if very amateur, 'archaeologists' who were guests of a nearby hotel.) It is probably stretching the point to call Sint Eustatius a time capsule, left behind by all those plantation owners and their slaves, the many fabulously rich merchants, the numerous occupying soldiers, and the thousands of seamen from the ships of all nations who lived on or visited the island during the eighteenth century. But because of its peculiar history, with the island losing the majority of its population within the first quarter of the next century, there surely remains much of the past waiting to be discovered, explored, researched, classified and catalogued.

There is a great deal to interest amateur historians, archaeologists, anthropologists and sociologists alike. The traveller looking for an island in the Caribbean, but one outside the normal concept of a Caribbean tourist resort, will enjoy Sint Eustatius. It offers something special, but probably will only appeal to a special sort of visitor. With its fairly rugged coastline and volcanic origin it has few beaches, and these of course are made of black sand. It can provide few of the standard vacation attractions although there are two beach hotels. Other than **La Maison sur la Plage** at the northern end of Concordia Bay on the otherwise deserted north-east coast, and **The Old Gin House** on Oranje Bay, accommodation is limited to a few guest-houses and apartments in or around Oranjestad.

Oranjestad

Fort Oranje is the focal point of the town and incorporates the oldest building on the island. It is situated on the edge of the cliff overlooking Oranje Bay about 40 m above the sea, with a commanding view of the western approaches to the island. The fort has been extensively restored and part of the pleasure of a visit is in seeing that the various buildings inside the stout walls are still in use today as they were in the past. It is still the administrative centre of the island. Within a few minutes' walk is a small and well-

Fort Oranje

kept museum. This is housed in what is always referred to as '**de Graaff's house**', after the commander who, in 1776, authorized the famous salute to the Great Union flag. It is not clear why it is called by this name as de Graaff never lived there. It was used by Admiral Rodney during his brief stay in 1781, but considering what he did for Sint Eustatius it seems highly unlikely that the house will ever be renamed. As it is over 200 years old it is as much part of the history of the island as the exhibits displayed inside.

The ruins of the **Honen Dalim Synagogue** are very close to the town square (which in fact is not a square at all, but merely a wide part of the main street, but none the less easily identifiable as the

The ruins of Honen Dalim Synagogue, Oranjestad

centre of the town). The yellow brick walls are all that remain of a substantial two-storey building built between 1739 and 1772, and which on completion had a brief existence as a synagogue. Within ten years of it being finished the Jewish community, which had grown rapidly during the island's golden era, was one of the prime targets for the wrath of Rodney. The Jewish merchants were driven out of business and many left the island. The last Jew died in 1846 and Honen Dalim ('she who is charitable to the poor') by that time had fallen into complete disrepair. Today, although some of the attraction has been lost because of a very commonplace house built immediately alongside them, the remains warrant a visit — even if only to compare them with the more substantial ruins of the **Dutch Reformed Church** situated beside Fort Oranje.

This church was begun in 1774 mainly because those merchants who were members of the Dutch Reformed Church had no wish to be outdone by their Jewish competitors. It took considerably less time to build than the synagogue but lasted no longer in service. Once again Rodney was the man responsible for its ultimate destruction. After the events of 1781 and the enormous disruption of all commercial activity many of the Christian merchants also

The ruins of the Dutch Reformed Church, Oranjestad

joined the exodus. The minister of the church followed them in 1792 and the building was abandoned. An attempt was made to revive the church some sixty or so years later. In the light of the Dutch Reformed Church's well-known views on race, and considering that by that time the majority of the island's inhabitants were black, it is hardly surprising that this met with no success. The square tower of the church has been restored and is now open to the public, but the remainder of the building is open to the sky. The surrounding burial ground contains some excellent examples of the local barrel-vault tombs, including that of another of the eighteenth century commanders, Jan de Windt, who died in 1775.

Forts and walks

Commander de Windt had a hand, as will be seen, in constructing some of the island's defences, but a great deal of work on the fortification of Sint Eustatius was carried out by the French during their fourth occupation between 1781 and 1784. By the end of the eighteenth century at least 14 forts or batteries had been built all around the island. Many never amounted to very much, and probably they were never all manned at the same time. They were certainly all quite useless in preventing the island from being attacked and seized. At present less than half of them are easily accessible and visited regularly. The remainder, while very little of them may remain above the ground, have yet to be investigated and explored — and in one or two cases even to be located.

One way of possibly rediscovering these old fortifications is by walking around the island. The general terrain is ideal for hiking and a number of 'nature trails' have been established by the Tourist Department, both through the northern hills and around The Quill. These range from easy one-hour strolls to lengthy treks which are, as the Tourist Department brochure puts it, 'not recommended unless you are an experienced mountaineer'. The toughest and possibly most rewarding is a trail leading up to the crater of **The Quill**, although this hardly demands mountaineering experience. Once at the rim of the crater, which is about 760 m in diameter and over 300 m deep, it is possible to walk most of the way around it or follow a trail to the bottom. Inside is a luxuriant rain forest, dark and moist, rising from ground covered with mosses, ferns and decaying vegetation. The trees are mostly cotton, mahogany and breadfruit, with lots of arums, bromeliads, lianas and orchids. Although the forest is only a miniature version of the kind found covering large areas of some of the islands further south in the eastern Caribbean chain, the mere fact that such a place should exist on an island like Sint Eustatius — which everywhere else is covered with thorny scrub — makes the effort to see it well worth while. The track which leads around the rim eventually reaches the highest point, called **Mazinga,** on the eastern side. From there the view alone makes all the discomfort of the long, hot climb fade into insignificance.

It is also possible to follow a road, and then a track, all the way around the lower slopes of The Quill. On the southern side the track leads across the top of a most unusual and distinctive geological feature known as the **White Wall**. This is a colossal slab of limestone rising out of the sea and lying at a steep angle against the side of the volcano. It is at least 250 m high and can be identified quite clearly from 30 km or more away at sea. It is part of an underwater bed of coral which was lifted out of the sea and then tilted by immense volcanic forces. This probably happened long after The Quill was first formed and shortly, in geological terms, before the volcano became extinct. Another good view of it is obtained from the partially restored ruins of **Fort de Windt** at the end of the road leading along the south coast from Oranjestad. This fort was built in 1753 and is named after the commander who was buried in the grounds of the Dutch Reformed Church two years later. From the ruins the island of St Kitts can be seen very clearly to the south-east across what is sometimes called The Channel. The prominent citadel of **Brimstone Hill** near the northern end, together with the lush green fields of sugar-cane rising up the lower slopes of **Mount Liamuiga,** provide sharp contrasts with the meagre remains of Fort de Windt and the surrounding barren hillside. One can only assume that de Windt's decision to build his little battery almost within the shadow of the immensely superior fortifications of Brimstone Hill was his way of cocking a snook (an English expression of Dutch origin if ever there was one) at his more powerful neighbour.

Sint Eustatius' other neighbour, a little further away than St

Kitts in the opposite direction, needed no such gesture of defiance — if such it was. By looking to the north-west from the battlements of Fort Oranje the outline of another mountainous island can be seen. The blue-grey peak, rising out of the blue Caribbean, has an almost mystical appearance. From such a distance it is difficult to imagine it being inhabited, and one half expects it to disappear if approached — the Caribbean equivalent of one of the fabled islands of the South Pacific reported by the early explorers but never seen again. This vaguely supernatural appearance may have had more than a passing relevance in the distant past. Among the Amerindians small images made of stone or other materials, which were called *zemis,* were treated as gods. Judging by the many examples discovered throughout the region the triangular or three-pointed variety seems to have been the most important. From certain directions at a distance this island looks not unlike a three-pointed *zemi.* For this reason it is felt among some authorities now studying the Amerindian history of the islands, that this particular one may have had great religious significance for the early inhabitants of the entire region. Whether or not this was so is something for archaeologists and anthropologists to decide. What cannot be disputed is that today, no less than yesterday, Saba is a very special island unlike any other in the Caribbean.

Chapter 9

The incomparable island —Saba

The island

Saba is the northernmost of the volcanic islands of the eastern Caribbean, which begin at Grenada, over 600 km to the south. It is very small, about 13 square kilometres in area, and almost circular in shape. From the 870 m elevation of **Mount Scenery** in the middle of the island the land falls steeply into the sea on every side. These slopes are divided by 'guts' which contain streams when it rains. Otherwise Saba, like all the other islands, has no permanent running water. The sea all around is very deep, falling to over 500 m within the same distance of the shore in places. There are one or two small islets close to the northern side, otherwise the inshore waters are free of any dangers to navigation to within a few metres of the coast.

Because of the extremely rugged coastline and the absence of sheltered bays, landing on Saba has always been difficult. Even today, after the construction of a small airstrip and an equally small harbour on opposite sides of the island, landing is not something which can be achieved on every day of the year, or without a missed heartbeat from time to time. The lower slopes of the island, especially on the drier leeward side, are fairly barren and covered with low bush and scrub. The vegetation increases with altitude and the upper part, to the top of Mount Scenery, is thickly wooded. All the human communities are at 300 to 400 m above the sea. In the past this made life extremely difficult for the inhabitants who had to carry everything (including even fresh water to one community) up from sea-level. At the same time it rendered them safe from attackers and throughout its history Saba was rarely stormed with any success. When it changed hands it was usually only because the other Dutch islands had done so.

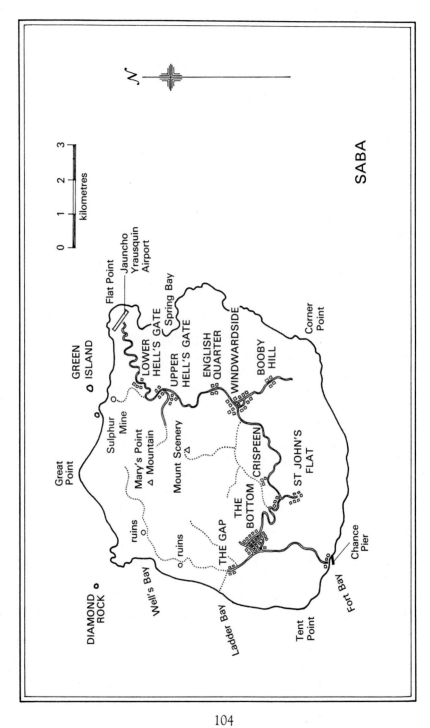

SABA

Saba from the south

Discovery and settlement

Saba may have been inhabited from time to time in the distant past by the Amerindians, but nothing has been discovered which pre-dates AD 800. The Carib word for rock was *siba*, and this seems the most likely origin of the island's present name. The fact that *zemis* made from a type of rock found only in Saba have been discovered in other islands adds weight to the theory that the island had a peculiar religious significance for the early peoples of this region. It was discovered by Columbus on the same day that he sighted Sint Eustatius. He gave it the name St Cristobal, but this was later transferred to the present island of St Christopher (St Kitts) for reasons which are now obscure.

Neither Columbus nor any of the Spanish settlers who followed him to the Caribbean attempted to settle on the island. Anyone who sails around it today will understand the reasons for this. From every direction the appearance (ignoring the present signs of life and habitation) is forbidding and landing apparently impossible. Some English sailors who were wrecked there in 1632 found it uninhabited. After their rescue it remained unoccupied for another eight years before Dutch settlers, originally from Zeeland, arrived from Sint Eustatius. These were soon joined by people from the British Isles, most of them presumably having some pressing reason for leaving one or other of the British islands near by. By 1665 the population of about 250 was made up of people from the Netherlands, England, Ireland and Scotland, but all owing allegiance to the Dutch throne. In that same year it was captured by the British — the first of numerous changes of ownership which took place for the next 150 years. All the inhabitants except 54 Englishmen were deported. Few of those deported ever returned and there is little evidence that Dutch people ever came to Saba in large numbers. The present white inhabitants are most likely descended from, in the main, people from the British Isles. The black Sabans of course are the descendants of slaves imported during the seventeenth and eighteenth centuries. In 1700, when the population had risen to over 500, one third were slaves.

Because of the incredible topography it was a struggle for anyone to survive on the island. The usual West Indian master and slave relationship based on the plantation system was never established. There were always more whites than blacks, and both master and slave must have lived under much the same conditions in the early days. To survive both had to work the land, so any unduly harsh treatment of the slave by the master would have been self-defeating. By the time the Netherlands Government got around to emancipating slaves in 1863 the blacks numbered only about one third of the total population of 1800.

The first settlement was made at **Fort Bay**, a minute indentation on the south-west coast. This must have seemed a most precarious foothold, with the sea crashing against the rocks on one side, and the towering slope of the mountain on the other. One can only marvel at the persistence and pugnacity of those first inhabitants in their determination to force an existence from such a forbidding island. The view from sea-level, whether ashore or near the coast at sea, remains daunting. It improves with altitude and as the interior is revealed. That this initial settlement was destroyed by a landslide was probably all to the good, as it forced the settlers to take to the hills, literally. Once the habitation known as **The Bottom** had been established they were safe from attackers, and had access to reasonably fertile ground. It was called The Bottom possibly because it was thought that the large depression in which

The Bottom

it was built was the bottom of a crater, although an alternative explanation is that the name is derived from the Dutch word for a bowl. Whatever the derivation The Bottom has remained the principal community on Saba until today.

Developing the island

As other communities were established they acquired names which were equally basic and descriptive, among them **Upper** and **Lower Hell's Gate**, **Windwardside**, **English Quarter**, **St John's Flat**, **The Gap** and **The Level**. The people who inhabited them depended on farming and fishing for their livelihood. Towards the end of the seventeenth century the Sabans became well known in the region for producing shoes and boots. Even though this industry died during the next century there still remains a faint

Windwardside

echo of it; the small group of houses called **Crispeen** half-way between Windwardside and The Bottom was undoubtedly named after the patron saint of shoemakers, St Crispin.

The Saba Bank, just to the south-west, has always provided good fishing, and may well have been one of the main reasons why the island was settled in the first place. The Saban men soon established a reputation as good seamen, and this led to the start of a boat-building industry along the foreshore of the slightly more protected south-west coast. At the close of the last century Saba had a fishing fleet of over 20 boats, some of which were large enough to work for lengthy periods around the small islands off the coast of Venezuela. Many of these boats were built on Saba. By that time, too, various Sabans owned sizeable schooners. The island's skippers and seamen were known and respected throughout the eastern Caribbean, trading between the US Virgin Islands in the north and what used to be British Guiana, now Guyana, in the south.

The population grew steadily from the time of the first settlement, passing the one thousand mark in the middle of the eighteenth century and reaching 2000 around 1880. It reached its peak of nearly 2500 in 1915. This was probably more people than such a small island could reasonably support, and when the first oil refineries opened up in Curaçao and Aruba a few years later emigration to these larger islands saved the day. The population declined for the next 40 years or more until, in about 1960, it fell to less than 1000 again — of whom there were many more women than men. The figure is little more than this today, but the ratio of the sexes is probably more evenly balanced.

Saba, like the other four islands, has been transformed during the last quarter of a century. In the other islands this was brought about largely by outside forces acting on the inhabitants, such as the demands of the tourist industry, or through some sort of political pressure being brought to bear on the governments of the countries that own them. In Saba the transformation has been brought about mostly through the efforts of the Sabans themselves, and is even more remarkable considering the number of people available during this period to bring it into effect. These efforts started in the early 1940s when the first stretch of road was built on the island between Fort Bay and The Bottom. This road, which is just over one kilometre in length, took five years to construct. When the first motorized vehicle, a Jeep, was landed in 1947 this was the only stretch of road on which it could operate. It took until 1960 for a road to be made from The Bottom to Hell's Gate — which are less than 5 km apart. Only those who see these roads can appreciate the effort involved in their construction with the very limited amount of plant and equipment available to their makers. By 1960 there were about twelve vehicles on the island; today there are 200 or more, and this figure includes three or four for rental. That any are needed for hiring out is due entirely to an event which took place in 1959.

Landing on Saba

In February of that year a small private aircraft, flown by the intrepid Remy de Haenen, landed on a rough airstrip prepared by the Sabans on Flat Point, at the north-eastern corner of the island. Flat Point is the seaward end of the greatest lava flow from Mount Scenery and the only sizeable area of level ground on the island.

Even then it is probably no more than 7 hectares in extent. This landing opened the way to the construction of the present airport in 1963. Named after **Juancho Yrausquin** (the Minister of Finance in the Government of the Netherlands Antilles at the time) it has a single runway 400 m in length, and what must be one of the world's smallest air terminals. The provision of an airstrip opened the island to the outside world. Before it was built Saba could only be reached by sea, and sea traffic consisted of a monthly supply ship, a weekly mail schooner, and one or two launches which operated an *ad hoc* service with Sint Maarten. Not surprisingly visitors were uncommon and before 1963 tourists numbered no more than two or three hundred a year. Once the airport was opened the numbers started to increase, and today up to 8000 tourists fly to Saba annually.

Spring Bay

These visitors experience a dramatic arrival. The flight from Sint Maarten takes about 15 minutes, and the service is operated by aircraft specifically designed to land and take off in a short space. The plane flies directly towards, and to within about 500 m of the precipitous north coast, before banking sharply and dropping down on to what, through the cockpit window, looks like the flight deck of a stationary and exceedingly small aircraft-carrier. That the plane requires less than half of the length of the airstrip to complete its landing is apparent only to those who can bear to keep their eyes open throughout.

Once on the ground and out of the aircraft the true nature of the terrain can be appreciated for the first time. The tiny airport building is at the foot of a steep slope leading directly to the summit of Mount Scenery some 800 m above. The village of Hell's Gate can be seen as some white dots seemingly about half-way up. It is joined to the airport forecourt by a road of the sort normally found only in the highest Swiss canton or leading to one of the remoter Greek monasteries. It is built to the same excellent standard as the rest of the island's road system, and provides a true test of a driver's skill. It also provides an equally searching test of his vehicle's transmission and gearbox. The total length of road on the island can be no more than 10 or 11 km. To traverse it requires the use of the first two gears for about 95 per cent of the time. In the light of these facts it is difficult to believe that the few self-drive rental cars are in great demand.

Prior to 1972, for those visiting Saba by sea, landing from the ship or launch was not without some risk. With no harbour or jetty all passengers and cargo had to be brought ashore in small boats, either in Fort Bay or, if sea conditions were too rough there, in Ladder Bay on the west coast. Landing on the west coast can never have been a welcome experience; that side of the island is so steep that the only way of climbing from the beach to The Bottom was by means of a flight of over 500 steps. This daunting prospect changed in 1972 when a small harbour was created at Fort Bay by building a pier. It is about 80 m in length and is named after **Captain L A I Chance,** the Saban who was largely responsible for getting it built. It is in regular use by the coasters and launches which bring supplies to the island, and also by one or two of the smaller Caribbean cruise ships. The number of tourists arriving

111

by sea has increased considerably since the port was opened, and Saba now expects up to 6000 such visitors each year. Private yachts calling at the island average about 250 a year. This is a very low figure compared with the other islands but the Chance pier is not a very suitable berth for yachts, on account of the swell which is normally present, and anchorages are uncomfortable for the same reason.

As already pointed out in Chapter 4, perhaps the simplest way for a yachtsman to visit Saba is for him to leave his boat at secure moorings in Great Bay and fly over from Sint Maarten. The daily flights to and from Saba are scheduled to allow the day visitor about seven hours on the island. Accommodation for those who want to spend more time there is mostly at Windwardside, but there is also a guest-house in The Bottom and a number of apartments in Hell's Gate. Other than the charming **Captain's Quarters Hotel** and the self-designated 'cheap 'n' cheerful' **Scout's Place** guest-house, the accommodation in Windwardside consists of self-catering houses, cottages and apartments.

The Captain's Quarters Hotel

Exploring Saba

A tour of the island by car can be completed in a couple of hours, even allowing for 'camera stops' and the fact that the speed of driving is unlikely to exceed 15 km per hour. Some of the views, which are come upon totally unexpectedly because of the incredible terrain, are breath-takingly beautiful. The more the island is explored the harder it becomes to understand how people could not only have settled there in the first place, but then have made it so idyllic. The road system is still being extended. It is possible to drive about two-thirds of the way to the top of Mount Scenery using a road from Hell's Gate, and it is planned that this will eventually link with a road from the south somewhere on the western side of the mountain. Yet another road is being constructed from The Bottom to Well's Bay in the north-west. It is thought that this bay will afford a better anchorage for ships than either Fort Bay or Ladder Bay, and will enable cruise ship passengers to be landed in comparatively calm conditions.

But Saba is a place which needs to be explored on foot, and there are tracks and trails leading to every part of the island. Probably the most popular is that from Windwardside to the top of Mount Scenery. This involves climbing over 1000 steps and passing through the lush vegetation of a tropical rain forest. Unfortunately for the visitor who is on the island for only one day, the top is frequently covered by cloud which can come and go with remarkable speed. It produces ideal conditions for the growth of the forest, but its development just as the perspiring climber reaches the 999th step can be a source of irritation.

A trail in the north, from near Lower Hell's Gate, leads to some old mine workings in the area known as **Behind the Ridge.** Sulphur was mined here briefly in the 1870s and again early in the present century for a year or two. Various tunnels and shafts are still to be seen. The reason that the mines were never worked with any great success becomes only too obvious on seeing where they are situated, and imagining how difficult it must have been to transport the sulphur to where it could be shipped. Another, much longer track, leads from The Bottom around the western side of the island. The first part is being made into the road to Well's Bay. This trail leads to the remains of two abandoned villages

113

The Sacred Heart Church, The Bottom

called **Middle Island** and **Mary's Point,** and then on into the heart of the remotest corner of Saba on the northern slopes of **Mary's Point Mountain.** In contrast to this, it is possible to follow another path through the most developed part of the island. This consists of a series of tracks and flights of steps which lead from Windwardside to The Bottom, and which were used by generations of Sabans before the motor road was constructed.

There were never any forts or fortifications in Saba and so the island has nothing resembling the ruins of Sint Eustatius. The only old building open to the public is a house in Windwardside which used to be the home of one of the many Saban men who spent most of their lives at sea earlier this century. It is now the **Saba Museum,** furnished just as it was when it was occupied, and housing a small but most interesting collection of Saban *memorabilia.* That the collection is not larger is no doubt due to the fact that the vast majority of houses which contain equally interesting antiques and curiosities are all still very much in use as family dwellings. In many ways all of Saba, with its neat houses with their red roofs, brightly painted doors and shutters, well-kept gardens and picket fences, is a living museum. Some of the gardens contain one or two barrel-vault tombs. These 'hurricane graves', as they are called, are designed to withstand high winds. Their presence, so near the houses of the living, seems neither morbid nor unnatural, and only reinforces the air of timelessness which surrounds Saba.

Typical Saban houses

'Spanish Work' and *Saban Spice*

The island produces two things which, other than its people, have achieved recognition in the outside world. These are the exquisitely embroidered 'drawn thread work' articles, and the *Saban Spice* liqueur — both produced by the ladies of Saba. The embroidery, often called 'Spanish Work', has been handed down from mother to daughter for the past hundred years. It was introduced by a teacher who was herself taught the art in a Venezuelan convent as a schoolgirl. By the early years of this century enough women knew how to do the work to begin trying to sell articles abroad. They established contact with prospective buyers, mostly in the USA, by writing to the manufacturers of products imported into Saba, and asking for the embroidery to be advertised amongst the firms' workers. In this way each individual slowly acquired her own clientele, and a steady export business grew up. As a result of one or two articles in national magazines in

'Spanish work'

the United States during the 1920s the trade was given a big boost, but this fell off as the USA entered the Depression. The demand for drawn thread work did not pick up again until after the airport was opened and tourists arrived looking for souvenirs. It is now a firmly established and profitable cottage industry, and no visitor can fail to be made aware of it. Many homes are open with a great variety of work on display, and visiting them offers a fascinating insight into Saban family life. The work involves incredibly neat and intricate stitching on shirts, blouses, pillowcases, table-cloths and many other items. Some ladies specialize in a particular sort of article, and no two offer identical pieces of work for sale.

Many of the embroiderers also make the celebrated local liqueur called *Saban Spice*. The origin of this is not so well known as that of the 'Spanish Work'. It probably began as an individual's recipe for a drink just called 'Spice' sometime in the eighteenth century. It is made of powdered aniseed, cloves and cinnamon boiled in a syrup of sugar and water. This mixture then has rum poured over it before it is strained. Once this has been done a certain proportion of the rum is burnt off to give the drink its peculiar smoky flavour before it is bottled. In days gone by most West Indian islands had a local drink of this nature — prepared to a time-honoured recipe using readily available ingredients. Perhaps the best-known example is one from Jamaica. What started off as, in this case, one family's concoction is now marketed commercially — and very successfully — as *Tia Maria*. Although *Saban Spice* is now bottled and labelled in a reasonably professional way it is still very much an individual product, and the taste will vary slightly between bottlers. Given the ingrained independence and individuality of the Saban people this is exactly as it should be.

The incomparable island

Perhaps what makes the biggest difference between Saba and the other islands is that the Sabans did not suffer the same reversal in fortunes as the people of all the others. The titular changes in ownership during the eighteenth century had little effect on the lives of the Sabans, who went about their main business of trying to extract a living under very difficult natural conditions. While many were forced to leave during the early years of the twentieth century in order to find work, they did not forget the island. A lot of the money they earned was used to maintain family homes and property. All the modern improvements — roads, vehicles, electricity, an airport and a landing pier — have come about because of the islanders' determination to develop their homeland in the face of many natural, and not a few man-made, obstacles.

The island is maintained in an almost immaculate condition. By any standards, especially West Indian ones, it is incredibly neat and tidy — but this is not to say that orderliness is taken to extremes. There is (or in 1985 there was) at least one derelict car beside the road, conveniently left in the one place on the entire island where it does not obstruct traffic. There is also at least one example of the other West Indian canker — the half-finished and abandoned building made of concrete blocks. But these are merely the Saban equivalents of the tiny deliberate mistakes which medieval craftsmen put into their work, in the belief that perfection was the prerogative of the Almighty. Saba was always a beautiful island, and must be one of the very few which has lost none of its beauty with the coming of man.

In spite of the severe hardships of life in earlier times, and the pressures of the modern world which now threaten, the inhabitants have created a society, a way of life and a habitat which all seem to be in complete harmony with nature. A traffic jam here is when one car has to wait while the driver of another exchanges greetings with a friend. It is a place where there are no cocks which insist on crowing throughout the day, and no dog is allowed to bark all through the night. It is a place where jet engines, police sirens, 'ghetto blasters', and other sources of aural pollution are unknown. It is a place where true peace and quiet complement the stupendous views from Booby Hill, The Level, Upper Hell's Gate and, if the cloud does not catch you, Mount Scenery. Saba is a place which is not only unlike any of the other islands but, in a much wider context, is quite incomparable.